Nizar Kabbani

Republic of Love

By far the most popular poet of the Arab World, the late Nizar Kabbani's selected poems appear here in English for the first time. So popular is he that one of his poems is the greatest love song in the Arab world, recorded by the legendary Egyptian singer Um Khalsoum and played on virtually every taxi's radio across the Middle East.

Nizar Kabbani (1923-1998) started writing at age 16; at 21 he published his first collection of love poems. Kabbani is the most read contemporary Arab poet. He was dubbed the Women's poet, the Homeland Poet, the Mamarian Poet, the Poet of Love, the Erotic Poet, the Feminist's Poet among other sobriquets, and is often regarded as *the* Arab poet of the twentieth century.

Nizar Kabbani

Republic of Love

Selected Poems in English and Arabic

Translated from the Arabic by Nayef al-Kalali
Edited by Lisa Kavchak

LONDON AND NEW YORK

First published in 2003 by
Kegan Paul International

This edition first published in 2010 by
Routledge
2 Park Square, Milton Park, Abingdon, Oxfordshire OX14 4RN

Simultaneously published in the USA and Canada
by Routledge
711 Third Avenue, New York, NY 10017, USA

First issued in paperbck 2016

Routledge is an imprint of the Taylor & Francis Group, an informa business

British Library Cataloguing in Publication Data
A catalogue record for this book is available from the British Library

Publisher's Note
The publisher has gone to great lengths to ensure the quality of this reprint but points out that some imperfections in the original copies may be apparent. The publisher has made every effort to contact original copyright holders and would welcome correspondence from those they have been unable to trace.

ISBN 13: 978-1-138-98519-3 (pbk)
ISBN 13: 978-0-7103-0680-7 (hbk)

To Salma…
Who helped with heart and hand

Posthumous Note

Being so fond of Kabbani and his writings, I hoped that this great man would live to view my translation of his work. However, his untimely death has sadly precluded me from fulfilling this ambition. My only consolation is that he did see the manuscript, made his comments, and approved it in principle.

It is my most sincere hope that the wealth of literature Nizar Kabbani bequeathed will remain, through these translations, a source of enlightenment for many generations to come.

Nayef al-Kalali
Bahrain

CONTENTS

Translator's Foreword

Much of Kabbani's poetry in this collection has been chosen for its merit as literature. My choice was guided by the belief that a translator does best in translating what he has enjoyed. Therefore, these poems may not necessarily be Kabbani's favourites. Though Kabbani himself aided in the selection of these poems, he once said, "Picking thirty flowers from a garden, and placing them in a vase is an act of great injustice against the garden."

Kabbani has conquered the Arab world with words. Anyone who reads him in Arabic must admire the splendour of his rhetoric, the luxuriance of his imagination, and the energy and aptness of his diction. Yet, to capture all the flavour of these qualities in a translation would be an attempt to create an art of the impossible.

To my knowledge, there have been a few translated books of Nizar Kabbani's poems. I have perused three; most notably the first English–language collection entitled *Arabian Love Poems* by Bassam Frangieh and Clementina Brown, which Kabbani himself gave me for use as a reference.

I began this project by myself, but later found that without the help of a proper editor, I couldn't have completed the project. As I am a civil engineer by profession, I bore in mind the Arabic proverb "Let the bread be made by the baker even if he eats half of it", when I undertook this project.

That is to say, the labourer is worthy of his hire. Lisa Kavchak was then introduced to me by Dr Abdul Aziz Bulaila, an Arabian Gulf University professor of English Literature. Her contribution to this book in editing and "trans–creating" was invaluable. I already knew that Kabbani wanted his translators to be creative, to "trans–create" rather than plainly translate.

Since this is my first book, a number of difficulties have arisen during the translation. Cross–cultural differences, unsuitable literal translation, the flow of the English text (although metre and rhyme are sacrificed) are but few of the difficulties I encountered. For instance, in the poem "Vessels Of Pus", Kabbani describes how a woman might express her sexual hunger when the man close to her did not satisfy her, portraying the man literally as an *igloo*. However, igloo wasn't particularly poetic and did not relate to the previous descriptions (Murderer, Pirate) of the man who had turned his back on her, so I considered using the word *cold–hearted man* or *frigid man* instead.

Another difficulty I encountered was in identifying certain Arab characters to the English–speaking reader. In order to render the poems in readable English and to be faithful to the original tone, meaning, and atmosphere, in certain cases, I replaced these characters with simple descriptions in English. The *Black Knight* was the identity given to *Antara al-Absi* in the poem "A Letter To An Anonymous Man." In another poem,

"The Last Declaration Of King Schariar", the sobriquet *Mythical Lover* replaced *Qais ibn al-Mulawwah*, a character perhaps unknown to the non–native Arab reader, but similar to Romeo. I have given full explanations of these characters in the *Notes to the Poems* section.

Hence, I took the liberty of introducing several creative changes necessary to capture the essence of the original. Nevertheless, I retained the name of Harun al-Rashid in the poem "Painting With Words", rather than replacing it with a sobriquet like the *"Great Caliph"* or *"Merry King*", since this character is known to the non–Arab world. The Irish poet Yeats wrote a long poem entitled "The Gift of Harun al-Rashid" in his collection *W. B. Yeats – the Love Poems*.

A number of politically rebellious poems were omitted from the manuscript upon Kabbani's request. To him, certain poems were outdated, having made their point in time. Nonetheless, I have left one poem entitled "The Runners", which was written in 1995, for the curious reader to sample.

Acknowledgements

I wish to thank the former Information Attaché, Mr Adnan Yousif, at the Embassy of the State of Bahrain, London, for arranging the meeting with Mr Kabbani; Mr Emad A. R. al-Moayed for guidance throughout the project; Dr Fadhel al-Arrayed, Professor of Human Physiology, and Dr Abdul Aziz Bulaila, Assistant Professor of Literature, Bahrain University, for assisting the team in translation; Ms Khulood al-Murbati for typing the Arabic text; Ms Ciara Hunt, Ms Lisa Jackson, Ms Hana Malik, Ms Claire Askey, and Ms Katherine Collings for proof–reading excerpts from the draft translation; Scott Reid for his assistance in the final preparation of the manuscript; Ahlam Elias for the cover design assistance and the poet's daughter, Hadba Kabbani, for granting permission to publish this collection.

Special thanks go to **Dr. Ghazi A. R. al-Gosaibi** for his valuable subvention to print this book.

Nizar Kabbani: A Profile

"Now we may ask ourselves, what is a Poet? A Poet is a prophet, a philosopher, a painter, a musician and a priest in one." Mikhail Nuaima.

One of the Arab world's greatest poets, Nizar Kabbani was born in Damascus, Syria in 1923, and started writing poetry at 16 years of age. In 1944, he graduated from the Faculty of Law at Damascus University and went on to join the Syrian Foreign Ministry, occupying a number of diplomatic posts in Cairo, Ankara, London, Madrid, Beijing, and Beirut. He resigned from the diplomatic corps in 1966 and established his own publishing house in Beirut. It wasn't long afterward that he witnessed the death of his wife, Belquis, as a result of a bomb attack on the Iraqi Embassy in Beirut in 1981.

The civil war in Lebanon impelled the poet to move from Beirut to Switzerland in 1982. Later, he moved to London where he had a weekly column in the International Arabic daily *Al–Hayat*.

One of the most prolific, reactive writers, issuing more than forty collections of both poetry and prose, Nizar Kabbani produced collections of poems that often ran into six or seven impressions.

Nizar Kabbani has acquired tremendous popularity across the Arab world, primarily through his love poetry. He was able to make his poetic language simple and similar to the language of ordinary people.

Regarded as *the* Arab poet of the twentieth century, poetry to Nizar Kabbani was his "daily bread" which he prepared himself; it was a "popular scarf" worn by millions of Arabs.

With his innovative poetry, Kabbani mesmerised Arab masses of all castes and thus founded his own kind of "republic." They felt that he reflected their innermost sentiments in both love and politics, breaking down barriers of fear, reluctance and taboo that prevailed between poetry and people. Poetry is so utterly important in the lives of the Arabs that his poetry readings in the Arab cities turned into unusual cultural phenomena. Leading singers also hankered after his poetry collections to use as lyrics, thus securing high sales and popularity. Their songs often occupied top places in the Arabic music charts. Kabbani was at times reluctant to allow his words to be sung for they were written as poems, not lyrics.

He is always regarded primarily in the Arab world as a "women's poet", owing to his controversial pro–feminist works. Kabbani was candid about his obsession with the word breasts, and critics hence have long dubbed Nizar as the Poet of Breasts. He never listened to the flak of his critics. "Had I listened to my critics, I wouldn't have been Nizar Kabbani", he remarked.

Although his mammarian expressions are artistically rich, they might give the impression that the poet was a seducer or even worse, a "Schariar", that ruthless womanising king who seduced women at night and dumped them in acid the next morning. In his autobiography Kabbani said, "Whoever saw my bedroom would have noticed that it didn't accommodate more than a single bed, an ashtray, a table lamp, a pen and a notebook filled with unclear scribbles of uncompleted poems. I am not a professional in slaying beautiful women but indeed in venerating them. If you go back to my old love records, you would find that in my most emotional experiences, I was the slain and not the slayer, the slaughtered and not the slaughterer. In fact, more than one woman crushed me. More than one woman sold me out. More than one woman used me as a bridge to fame. More than one woman caged me like a bird to sing her praises and satisfy her narcissism or used me as a postman to deliver love letters to her, night and day."

According to the *Al–Khaleej* newspaper, Monday, 6 July 1998, Kabbani knew that many young lovers plagiarised his love poetry when they wrote passionate letters to their sweethearts. He added with a smile, "They admitted it to me and I forgive them for plagiarising me if it only made them happy." He continued laughingly, "A leading critic stated that there is no single lover in the Arab world who didn't send verses of Nizar Kabbani's poetry to his sweetheart."

A number of close relatives and acquaintances of Nizar, including his elder brother Mu'taz, revealed how the late poet led his life. Kabbani was more of the self–contained type. "He was born a poet and was dissimilar to us in the positive sense. More of the inquisitive type who pried for the truth and its minor details", said Mu'taz. Nizar was also a music lover and had a beautiful voice. He learnt how to play the lute and mastered composition. He relinquished all these hobbies later when he began his writing career. Nizar loved his domesticity. As a child and until the age of 12, Nizar never went out to play with the neighbourhood children. Even in his last ten years in London, Nizar remained a domestic person who didn't go out much except on a few occasions.

All the material that Kabbani has written on women and their bodies does not represent his actual experience. "Nizar Kabbani was never a seducer or a womaniser, as it may be perceived from his erotic poetry", his brother said. "I can attest that Nizar didn't love any woman in his life and did not have any girlfriends except for his late wife Balquis whom he wed for being a poetess", added his brother.

During his last ten years in London, his poems departed from the window of his Knightsbridge flat in a transcontinental flight onto the Arab streets. His long stay in the West had influenced his aspiration of achieving freedom and democracy in the Arab World, and thus inspired his patriotic poetry.

In his later years, Kabbani wrote a number of political essays and poems criticising various conditions. Kabbani noted, "The political verse was the last cure available in our hands to rescue the Arab body from semi–paralysis, immunodeficiency and national fragmentation." He envisioned that his role as a poet was "Injecting the Arab body with highly inflammable materials and stimulant drugs so that it remains on high alert with eyes wide–open and nerves high–strung."

Nizar Kabbani died from a heart attack in his London flat on Thursday, 30 April 1998. A special plane chartered by Syrian President Hafez al-Assad carried his remains to Damascus. More than half a million mourners walked in his funeral for ten kilometres to the cemetery. Around ten thousand people came from different parts of the Arab world and elsewhere to pay their respects. He was laid to rest in his hometown Damascus on Monday, 4 May 1998.

There are two reasons for translating poetry: To compare and to share. Firstly, I wanted to hear how these writers sounded in my own language, and secondly, I wanted others to be able to read them.

Octavio Paz

My deep poetic art the blind have eyes to see,
My verses ring in ears as deaf as deaf can be.
They wander far abroad whilst I am unaware,
But men collect them watchfully with toil and care.

Al-Mutannabi

Painting With Words

1966

Don't ask me for the record of my life.
It would be a long story,
my queen.
I have lived through all ages.
It's as if I have existed thousands of years.
My luggage is worn out
and I am exhausted from my adventures.
No ripe breasts, black or white,
are devoid of a sign of my conquests.
There remains no crevice within a fair lady's body
that lacks my trail marks.
I have tailored a gown out of
beautiful women's skin
and have built pyramids out of their nipples.
I have written poetry that is unparalleled,
except by God's words in the Old Testament.

*

Today I sit atop my ship
like a pirate espying an escape route.

الرَسْمُ بالكِلمَات

لا تطلبي منّي حسابَ حياتي
إنَّ الحديثَ يطولُ يا مولاتي !
كلُّ العصور أنا بها.. فكأنَّما
عمري ملايينٌ من السَنَواتِ
تعبتْ من السَّفرَ الطويل حقائبي
وتعبتُ من خيلي ومن غَزَواتي ..
لم يبقَ نهدٌ .. أسودٌ أو أبيضٌ
إلاَّ زرعتُ بأرضه راياتي ..
لم تبقَ زاويةٌ بجسم جميلةٍ
إلا ومرَّت فوقها عَربَاتي..
فصَّلتُ من جلد النساء عباءةً
وبنيتُ أهراماً من الحَلَماتِ
وكتبتُ شعراً .. لا يشابهُ سحرَهُ
إلا كلامُ اللّهِ في التَّوْراةِ ..

*

.. واليومَ أجلسُ فوقَ سطح سفينتي
كاللّص .. أبحثُ عن طريق نجاةِ

I try to use my traditional way of evasion –
through women.
Where are my concubines?
Where are the harems?
And where is the smell of incense
wafting through my chambers?
Today is the day the breasts
avenge themselves
and return my stabs.

*

Harun al-Rashid had such a bitter tragedy.
I wonder if you could imagine how bitter this
tragedy was.
I am just like a candle, my friend.
I weep,
but nobody notices my tears.
Sex to me was a temporary tranquilliser.
It did not end my sorrows or my crises,
and now love has become trite.
All kinds of love appear the same,
as indistinguishable as leaves in the forest.

وأُديرُ مفتاحَ الحريم .. فلا أرى
في الظلِّ غيرَ جماجمِ الأمواتِ
أينَ السبايا ؟ أينَ ما ملكتْ يدي؟
أين البَخُورُ يضوعُ من حُجُراتي؟
اليومَ تنتقمُ النهودُ لنفسها ..
وتردُّ لي الطَعَنات بالطَعَناتِ..

*

مأساةُ هارون الرشيد مريرةٌ
لو تدركينَ مرارةَ المأساةِ
إني كمصباح الطريق .. صديقتي
أبكي .. ولا أحدٌ يرى دَمَعاتي ..
الجنسُ كانَ مُسَكِّناً جرَّبْتُهُ
لم يُنْهِ أحزاني ولا أزَمَاتي
والحبُّ أصبَحَ كلّهُ متشابهاً
كتشابُهِ الأوراقِ في الغاباتِ ..

I am incapable of loving the minutest creature
or even the most inanimate of objects.
I have practised more than a thousand religions,
and have found the best religion is to
worship myself.
Your sweet mouth won't solve my predicament.
The answer to my dilemma lies within my
notebooks.
All the roads ahead are blocked;
our only salvation is in painting with words.

أنا عاجزٌ عن عشق أيّة نملةٍ
أو غيمةٍ .. عن عشق أيّ حصاةِ
مارستُ ألفَ عبادةٍ وعبادةٍ
فوجدتُ أفضلَها عبادةَ ذاتي

*

فَمُكِ المطيَّبُ.. لا يَحُلُّ قضيّتي
فقضيَّتي في دفتري ودَوَاتي
كلُّ الدروب أمامنا مسدودةٌ
وخلاصُنا .. في الرسم بالكلماتِ .

To A Saint

1961

What then do you expect,
you petty woman?
Answer me – what do you expect?
Should I stand here catching flies
while you smoke?
Should I regurgitate my dreams
like an addict
while lying in front of your neat bed
like a cuddly cat –
a clawless, honourless, decrepit cat?
I'll never be that kind of cat –
passionless and mummified,
dozing off while you undress
or offering to turn my head
when you remove your blouse
and reveal your mounds of jasmine.

*

What I just said doesn't surprise me at all,
so why do you look stunned?
This is me. This is who I am.
What are your latest demands now?

إلى قدِّيسَة ..

ماذا إذَنْ تتوقَّعينْ؟
يا بضْعَةَ امرأةٍ .. أجيبي
ما الذي تتوقَّعينْ؟
أأظلُّ أصطادُ الذبُابَ هُنا؟..
وأنتِ تُدَخّنينْ
أجْتَرُّ كالحشَّاشِ أحلامي
وأنتِ تُدَخّنينْ..
وأنا .. أمامَ سريركِ الزاهي ..
كقِطّ ٍ مستكينْ ..
ماتتْ مخالبُهُ ، وعِزَّتُهُ .. وهدَّتْهُ السنينْ
أنا لَنْ أكونَ – تأكَّدي –
القِطَّ الذي تتصوَّرينْ
قِطّاً من الخشَبِ المجوَّفِ ..
لا يحرّكُهُ الحنينْ ..
يغفو على الكُرسِيِّ إذْ تتجرَّدينْ
ويردُّ عينيْهِ ..
إذا انحسرتْ قِبابُ الياسمينْ ...

*

تلكَ النهايةُ ..
ليسَ تُدْهِشُني .. فما لكِ تُدْهَشينْ
هذا أنا ..
هذا الذي عندي .. فماذا تأمُرينْ؟

I'm having a nervous breakdown,
and you sit there oblivious, lost in a book.
Do you expect me to consent to a fast from
kissing – from passion?

I'm offering you my manhood.
What more could you ask for?
Forget about my wisdom and my goodness,
for I know they are worthless to you.

*

A hermit! Who was it that said I was last of the
hermits?
My dear saint,
I'm not the god you perceive me to be.
I'm just an ordinary man
with all the good and bad virtues of the man
who possesses the noble traits of the prophet,
the heresies of the infidel,
the innocence of children,
and the cruelty of the savage –

أعصابيَ احترقتْ ..
وأنتِ على سريركِ تقرأينْ ..
أأصومُ عن شَفَتَيْكِ؟
فوقَ رجولتي ما تطلبينْ
ما حِكمْتي ؟ ما طيبَتي ؟
هذا طعامُ الميّتينْ ..

*

مُتَصوّفٌ!
مَنْ قالَ ؟ إنّي آخِرُ المتصوّفينْ
أنا لستُ يا قدّيستي ..
الربَّ الذي تتخيَّلينْ
رجلٌ أنا كالآخرينْ ..
بطَهَارتي .. بِنَذَالتي ..
رجلٌ أنا كالآخرينْ ..
فيه مزايا الأنبياءِ ..
وفيه كُفْرُ الكافرينْ ..
وداعةُ الأطفال فيه .. وقَسْوةُ المُتَوَحّشينْ

just an ordinary man.
A man who loves, and when he does,
does it with all the passion of a man of forty.
If you could only understand
what forty means.
And what love at forty means.
Oh petty woman,
if you could only understand.

رَجُلٌ أنا .. كالآخرينْ
رَجُلٌ يُحبُّ – إذا أحَبَّ –
بكُلِّ عُنْفِ الأربعينْ
لو كنتِ يوماً تفهمينْ
ما الأربعونَ ؟
وما الذي يعنيه حُبُّ الأربعينْ ؟
يا بِضْعَةَ امرأةٍ ..
لو أنّكِ تفهمينْ ...

To My Student

1961

Say to me – even lie – even flattering words,
your muteness is killing me.
You are still an amateur
in the art of love;
oceans and mountains isolate us.
You are still unable to understand
that all men are children.
I refuse to be a clown,
a dwarf who can swindle with his words.
And if I were dumbstruck before your beauty,
silence is a virtue in the temple of grace.
Our words of passion lead love to the grave;
emotions are better said in silence.

*

The stories of romance have laid ruins on you.
They are nothing but mere myths.
Love is not a fairy tale
ending with the wedding
of the hero and heroine.

إلى تِلميذة

قُلْ لي – ولو كَذباً – كلاماً ناعماً
قد كادَ يقتلني بكَ التمثالُ
مازلتِ في فنّ المحبّة .. طفلةً
بيني وبينكِ أبْحُرٌ وجبالُ
لم تستطيعي – بعدُ – أن تتفهّمي
أنَّ الرجالَ جميعَهمْ .. أطفالُ
إني لأرفضُ أن أكون مهرّجاً
قَزْماً .. على كَلِماتهِ يحتالُ
فإذا وقفتُ أمام حسنكِ صامتاً
فالصمتُ في حَرَمِ الجمالِ .. جمالُ
كَلِماتُنا في الحبِّ .. تقتل حبّنا
إنَّ الحروفَ تموتُ حينَ تقالُ

*

قِصصُ الهوى قد أفسدتكِ .. فكلُّها
غيبوبةٌ .. وخرافةٌ .. وخيالُ
الحبُّ ليس روايةً شرقيةً
بختامها يتزوّج الأبطالُ

It is sailing
without a ship,
leaving the port knowing
we will never reach our destination.
It is the continuous trembling
of our hands;
the lingering of an unspoken question;
the stream of sorrows
running deep inside us
with vines and crops
growing on its sides.
It is these crises
which bind us together.
We perish
so that hopes prosper.
It is when we rage
against any trivial incident.
It is our despair
and our deadly doubts.
It is this hand that,
as we bend to kiss it,
murders us.

لكنهُ الإبحارُ دون سفينةٍ
وشعورُنا أنَّ الوصولَ محالُ
*
هو أن تظلَّ على الأصابع رعشةٌ
وعلى الشفاه المطبَقات سؤالُ
هو جدولُ الأحزان في أعماقنا
تنمو كرومٌ حوله , وغِلالُ
هو هذه الأزَماتُ تسحقنا معاً
فنموتُ نحنُ .. وتزهرُ الآمالُ
هو أن نثورَ لأيِّ شيءٍ تافهٍ
هو يأسُنا .. هو شكُّنا القتَّالُ
هو هذه الكفُّ التي تغتالُنا
ونقبِّلُ الكفَّ التي تغتالُ ..

In Spite
1961

In spite of all our conflicts
and all our resolutions
that we can't make it work,
in spite of the animosity,
the obstinacy
and inhibitions,
in spite of the absence of our smiles
and the lack of communication,
there must be a mystery
that unifies our destinies –
brings our footsteps closer
and blends you into me,
melting your warm hands with mine.

*

In spite of all our differences,
our unmatched temperaments,
the dark days of detachment
and the retrieval of all the gifts and photographs –

قِصّة خِلافَاتِنا

برَغْمِ .. برَغْمِ خلافاتِنا
برَغْمِ جميع قراراتِنا
بأنْ لا نعودْ
برَغْمِ العَدَاءِ .. برغْمِ الجَفَاءِ .
برَغْمِ البُرُودْ ..
برَغْمِ انطفاء ابتساماتِنا
برغْمِ انقطاع خطاباتِنا
فثمّةَ سرٌ خفيّ
يُوحّدُ ما بينَ أقدارنَا
ويُدْني مواطيءَ أقدامِنَا
ويُفنْيكِ فيْ
ويصهرُ نارَ يَدَيْكِ بنار يدّيْ ..
*
برغْمِ جميع خلافاتِنا
برغْمِ اختلاف مناخاتِنا
برغْمِ سُقُوط المَطَرْ ..
برغْمِ استعادة كُلّ الهدايا
وكُلّ الصُوَرْ ..
برغْمِ الإناءِ الجميل
الذي قلتِ عنهُ .. انكسَرْ

in spite of the dreariness,
I still believe
that destiny insists
on our togetherness
and rejects
all our arguments

*

In spite of the autumn of our relationship
and the bleeding going deep inside us,
in spite of our persistence
to put an end to our drama
at any cost,
in spite of our determination
that I won't
and you won't –
I doubt that we can.
In spite of all these conflicts,
we are helpless
in the face of our fate.

برغْمِ رَتَابَة ساعاتِنا
برغْمِ الضَجَرْ ..
فلا زلتُ أؤمنُ أنَّ القدَرْ
يُصِرُّ على جمع أجزائِنا
ويرفضُ كُلَّ اتهاماتِنا ..

*

برغْم خريف علاقاتِنا
برغْمِ النزيف بأعماقِنا
وإصرارنا ..
على وضع حدٍّ لمأساتِنا
بأيِّ ثَمَنْ ..
برغْمِ جميع ادِّعاءاتِنا
بأنّيَ لنْ ..
وأنَّكِ لَنْ ...
فإنّي أشُكُّ بإمكانِنا
فنحنُ برغْمِ خلافاتِنا
ضعيفانِ في وجه أقدارنا

How alike we are
in our spirits,
in our thoughts,
and even in our books and colours.
Isn't all of this
profound evidence
that we are friends of the same destiny,
travelling the same road
despite all our insanities?

شبيهانِ في كُلِّ أطوارنا
دفاترُنا ، لونُ أوراقِنا
وشَكْلُ يدينْا .. و أفكارنا
فحتَّى نقوشُ ستاراتِنا
وحتى اختيارُ اسطواناتِنا
دليلٌ عميقْ
على أننا ..
رفيقا مصير ، رفيقا طريقْ
برغْم جميع حماقاتِنا ..

Love Of 1994

1994

When I decided to make you my love,
I was neither democratic –
as I usually claim to be –
nor intellectual,
and not even civilised.
I was a man who had on his skin
the tattoos of the African tribes
and the heritage of a thousand years of Bedouin
life.

*

I don't believe in love through parliaments,
consultative councils or referendums.
I cannot love a woman through personal ads
or date lines.
It's I who decides whom I will love.
It's I who sketches her features and lineaments –
I decide the length of her hair,
the size of her waist.
And I design her breasts
according to my specifications.

حُبّ 1994

عندما صَمَّمْتُ أن أجعلَكِ حبيبتي
لم أكُنْ ديمُوقراطياً – كما أدَّعي –
ولا حضاريّاً – كما أدَّعي –
ولا مثقّفاً – كما أدَّعي–
وإنما كنتُ رَجُلاً يحملُ فوق جلِدهِ
وَشْمَ القبائل الإفريقيَّهْ ..
وميراثَ ألفِ عامٍ من البَداوَهْ ...

*

إنني لا أؤمِنُ بالحُبّ..
عن طريق البرلماناتْ
ومجالس الشُورى
والاستفتاءات الشعبيَّهْ
ولا يمكنني أن أُحِبَّ امرأةً بالمراسلَهْ .
أو بالطُرُق البيروقراطيَّهْ
فأنا الذي أقرّرُ من تكون حبيبتي
وأنا الذي أرسمُ تقاطيعَها كما أريدْ ..
وأُطيلُ شعرَها.. كما أُريدْ
وأُدَوْزِنُ خَصْرَها .. كما أُريدْ ..
وأُهَنْدِسُ نهدَها بالحَجْم الذي أُريدْ ..

How can I be
democratic and a passionate lover
at the same time?
How can I be water and fire,
partial and neutral,
wise and insane,
an African and a Swede,
a coup plotter and a fundamentalist?
And how does it happen
that while I blow up the world with each poem I write,
you alone emerge unscathed?

*

I don't want you to treat me like a dervish
who doesn't know the number
of moles on your back
and cannot excel in playing Mozart
down the length of your spine.

*

How can I work as a poet during the day
and a professor of theocracy at night?

كيف يمكنني
أن أكون ديموقراطياً وعاشقاً
في ذات الوقتْ ؟
كيف يمكنني أن أكونَ ماءً .. وناراً ؟
مُتَورِّطاً .. ومُحَايداً ..
حَكيماً .. ومجنوناً ..
إفريقيّاً .. وسويديّاً ..
إنقلابيّاً .. وأُصُوليّاً ..
كيف أُفجّرُ الدنيا مع كلّ قصيدةٍ أكتبُها .
ولا أُفَجِّركِ مَعَها ؟ ...

*

كيفَ يُمكنني ؟
أن أتعامَلَ معكِ كدرويش
لا يعرفُ عددَ الشامَات على ظَهْركْ ..
ولا يُجيدُ عَزْف موزارت
على عَمُودِكِ الفِقَريّ ؟؟

*

كيفَ يُمكنني ؟
أن أشتغلَ في النهار شاعراً ..
وفي الليلْ ،
أستاذاً في الفقْهِ الدُسْتوريّ ؟ ..

When I decided that you would be my love,
I didn't ask for your permission.
Love decided for me – and for you.
It didn't worry me
whether you said no or said yes,
because all your no's were melting like candles
under the flame of my lips,
and all your vows of chastity were falling
like sparrow's feathers
on my bed cover.

*

When your tongue floundered under my tongue
like a crimson fish,
I felt the gyration of the Red Sea.
My ship dove between
the ruby reefs
and the heatwaves of the equatorial.
I wasn't thinking of anything
except loving you –
that you were a fish that trembled joyfully in my hand.

عندما قرّرْتُ أن تكُوني لي ..
لم أسْألْكِ رأيَكِ
لأنَّ الحُبَّ كان يُقرّرُ عنكِ .. وعنّي ..
ولم يكن يعنيني
أن تقُولي (لا) .. أو تقولي (نَعَمْ) ..
فجميعُ لاءاتكِ كانتْ تذوبُ كالشمعْ
على حَرَارة فمي ..
وجميعُ قراراتك كانت تتساقطُ
كريش العصافيرْ
على غطاءِ سريري!!

*

عندما اختلجَ لسانُكِ تحت لساني
كسَمكَةٍ قرمُزيَّهْ ...
شعَرتُ بدُوار البحر الأحمَرْ
وغاصَتْ سفينتي
بين مرايا الياقُوتْ
وحرائق خَطِّ الإسْتوَاءْ ..
لم أكنْ أفكّرُ بأيّ شيءٍ ..
إلاّ بأنني أحبُّكْ ..
وبأنّكِ سمكتي التي تنطُّ بين أصابعي فَرَحاً ..

Why throw you back to sea
when you have entered my territorial waters
and sought refuge
in my heart?

*

Forgive me if I loved you so violently
and so madly,
for violence is my weapon to write
and my weapon when I love.
And madness is the last gold ring
I place on your fingers.
Forgive me if I did not flatter and fawn enough;
I discarded my diplomatic attire a long time ago,
and with it,
my awkward postures, my mannered language,
my artificial smile and my paper masks.

*

Forgive me if I did not observe table etiquette,
for I don't know how to embrace you
while wearing my tie,
or how to devour your love with knife and fork.

فلماذا أُعيدُكِ إلى البحرْ ؟
بعدما دخلتِ مياهي الإقليميَّةْ ..
وطلبتِ اللجوءَ السياسيَّ إلى صدري ؟؟

*

سامحيني .. إذا أحببتُكِ بكلِّ هذا العُنفْ ..
وبكلِّ هذا الجُنُونْ ..
فالعُنْفُ هو سلاحي في الكتابَهْ ..
كما هو سلاحي في العِشقْ ..
والجُنونُ هو آخرُ خاتمٍ من الذَهَبْ
أضعُهُ في إصْبَعِكْ ..
سامحيني .. إذا لم أكنْ دبلوماسيّاً معكِ ..
فلقد خلعتُ ملابسي الدبلوماسيَّةَ من زمانٍ بعيدْ .
وخلعتُ معها مواقفي المُنَشّاةْ ..
ولغتي المُنَشّاةْ ..
وضِحْكَتي المُنشّاةْ ..
وأقنعتي الوَرَقيَّهْ ..

*

سامحيني ..
إذا خالفتُ آدابَ الجُلُوس إلى المائدَهْ ..
فأنا لا أعرفُ
كيف أعانقُكِ بِرَبْطَة العُنُقِ السوداءْ ..
ولا أعرفُ كيف أقشّرُ تُفّاحَ يَدَيْكِ ..
بالشَوْكَةِ والسِكّينْ !!

When I wrote your name in my notebook
and placed parentheses around it,
I did it intuitively, instinctively, and innocently.
No one taught me how to love you;
I learned on my own
how the bee secretes its honey,
the breast its milk,
the silkworm its silk,
and the poem its music.

*

I had neither instruction manuals
nor romantic novels to teach me –
I knew instinctively
that when I mixed the elements
of fire and gold,
a woman was formed,
that when I placed an apple beside an apple,
her breasts would thrust out,
that when I put my hand on your hand,
the fruit would ripen and fall from the tree,
and that when I kissed you,
the earth would quiver.

*

عندما كتبتُ اسْمَكِ على دفتري
ووضعتُهُ بين قَوْسَيْنْ ..
كنتُ أتصرَّفُ بفطْرتي .. وحَدْسي .. وطُفُولتي .
ولم يُعلِّمْني أحدٌ كيفَ أُحِبُّكِ ..
وإنما علّمتُ نفسي ..
كما تُفْرزُ النَحْلةُ عَسَلَها ..
والثَدْيُ حليبَهْ ..
ودودةُ القَزِّ حريرَها ..
والقصيدةُ موسيقاها ...
*
لم يكنْ عندي كُتُبٌ أقرؤُها
ولا رواياتٌ عن أخبارِ العشْقِ والعاشقينْ ..
ولكنّني اكتشفتُ على الطبيعَهْ
كيفَ أعجُنُ النارَ بالذَهَبْ
فتتشكَّلُ امْرأهْ ...
وكيف أضعُ التُفَّاحةَ إلى جانب التُفَّاحَهْ
فيتكوَّنُ النهدانْ ..
وكيف أضعُ يدي على يدِكْ ..
فتتساقطُ الفاكهَهْ ..
وكيف أضعُ فمي على فَمِكْ ..
فتهتَزُّ الكرةُ الأرضيَّهْ!!
*

I go to meet you with open arms
and forget to retrieve them when I leave,
and you come to me with a full mouth
and leave with one lip.

*

My narcissism spirals
whenever I see the lessons of love
I read to you
printed on your mirrored body,
and my pride swells when I see that the one
who was my first–year student
has now become my instructor.

*

When I mounted you on my wild horse of poetry
and announced at a press conference
that you were my love,
the bullets came at me
from every direction:

أذهبُ إلى مَوْعدِكِ بذراعَين مَفْتُوحَتَيْنْ
فأنْسَاهُما عندَكِ ..
تأتينَ إلى موعدي بفمٍ كاملْ ..
وتعودينَ بنصفِ فَمْ..

*

تزدادُ نَرْجسيَّتي
كلّما رأيتُ دروسَ الحُبِّ التي قرأتُها عليكِ ..
مطبوعةً على مرايا جَسَدِكْ ..
تزدادُ كبريائي كلّما شعرتُ أنّ التي كانتْ تلميذتي
في أوّل السنة الدراسيَّهْ
أصبحتْ أُستاذتي ..
عندما خطفتُكِ على حصَان الشّعرْ
وأعلنتُ في مؤتمرٍ صحافيّ: أنّكِ حبيبتي
تساقطَ الرَصَاصُ عليَّ من كُلّ مكانْ

From the military barracks, cultural clubs,
the Ministry of Social Affairs, the Ministry of Education,
the cafés, bars, churches,
and the women's associations.
My head was wanted in the name of justice at any price.
What kind and whose justice is it
if it doesn't deem love the fairest judge?
Oh the renegade from the
domination of history
and the legislation of Cave People,
oh lady, who is irking from her preserved body
and postponed femininity,
you won't regret flying with me
in the skies of freedom,
for no bird has regretted being a master in freedom.

من الثكَنَات العسكريَّةِ، من الأندية الثقافيَّهْ
من وزارة الشؤون الاجتماعيَّةِ، من وزارة التربيَةْ
من المقاهي، من الحاناتِ، من المعابد، من الكنائسْ
من الجمعيّات النسائيّةِ .. تساقَطَ الرصَاصْ ..
كان رأسي مطلوباً للعدالة بأيِّ ثَمَنْ ..
أيّةُ عَدَالةٍ تطلُبُني؟
أليسَ الحبُّ هو أعدلَ العادلينْ؟؟
أيَّتُها الخارجةُ على سلطة التَاريخْ ..
وشريعةِ أهْلِ الكهفْ ..
أيَّتُها المتمَلْمِلةُ من جَسَدكِ المُعلَّبْ ..
وأنوثتكِ المؤجَّلهْ ..
لا تندمي على الطيران معي في سماء الحريَّةْ ..
فليسَ هناكَ عصفورٌ في العالَمْ
نَدِمَ يوماً على احتراف الحريَّهْ ..

Give Me Love, Turn Me Green

1997

Listen carefully.
Listen carefully.
This love ordeal I'm going through
happens only once in a lifetime.
An ordeal that is poetic, aquatic,
mystical and sensual,
glorious in its sadness,
and don't I always wear my sadness
as a perfume?

*

Hold me tightly.
I feel weightless, my lady,
as if my veins had dissolved
and my bones vaporised.
Wash your hair in the river of my madness.
But then, isn't the madness of love inexplicable?

*

إمْنَحيني الحُبَّ كَيْ أصبحَ أخْضرَ !!.

إسْمَعيني جيّداً
إسْمَعيني جيّداً
أنا في حالة عِشْق ... ربُمَّا لا تتكرَّرْ ...
حالةٍ شعْرية.مائيَّةٍ.صُوفيَّة.جِنسـيَّةٍ
حالةٍ رائَعةٍ في حُزْنها
وأنا دوماً بحُزْني أتَعطَّرْ ...
*
عَانقيني جيّداً ...
أنا في حال انْعدامِ الوزْنِ، يا سـيِّدتي
فعُرُوقي تَتَلاشَـىَ...
وعظامي تَتَبخَّرْ..
إغْسلي شَعْرَكِ في نَهر جُنَوني...
فجُنوَنُ الحُبِّ، شَـيءٌ لا يُفسَّرْ !!
*

Read me intensely.
I am always searching for an avid reader,
one who wears poems about her wrists
like bracelets
and sees the whole world
in the portrait of a poet.

*

Let me intoxicate you.
Let me intoxicate you.
Let me intoxicate you until the sea
is pink and runs like wine
in tones of yellow and grey.
How wonderful for a woman to lose her head,
to become intoxicated before the face of poetry.

*

I am at my best,
the peak of my virility.
And oh, how I am enjoying it!
So give me another chance to write history,
for history, my lady, does not recur.

*

إقْرأيني جيّداً...
فأنا أبحث عن قارئةٍ مَهْووسَةٍ
تَضَعُ الأشعار في معْصَمِها
مثلَ الأساورْ
وترى العالمَ مرسوُماً
على صُورةِ شاعرْ...
*
إسْكَري بي...
إسْكَري بي...
إسْكَري حتى يصيرَ البحرُ
ورديّاً.نبيذياً.رمادياً وأصفرْ...
كمْ جمِيلٌ أن تُضيعَ امرأةٌ عقلَها..
في حَضْرةِ الشعْر..وتسكرا!!
*
أنا في أجمَل حالاتي
وفي أزْهَى حَضَاراتي
وكم يُعجبني أن أتحضر
فامنحيني فُرصةً أخرى
لكي أكتُبَ التاريخَ...
فالتاريخُ – يا سّيدتي – لا يتكرَّرْ..
*

With love, I have changed the history of my time
just like I changed the history of females.
For what's the value of poetry
if it doesn't have the power of change?
And what's a poet if he can't command change?

*

You who arrived in my mind
from the whiteness of jasmine,
from the spas of Granada
and the sorrows of the mandolin,
what can we possibly do?
The piano is drowning in its tears.
All the ports have closed,
and the marina's wine runs red.
I don't have a guidebook for love.
One day it's a flower I wear on my jacket,
on another, it's a dagger hidden in our bed,
on another, it's a flame that sears.
Still, on another, it's a sugar cube
dissolving sweetly on my tongue.

*

إنّني بالحُبّ... غَيَّرتُ زَمَاني
مثلما غيرّتُ تاريخَ الأُنوثهْ...
ما هو الشعرُ إذا لم يُغِيّرْ؟..
َمنْ هو الشاعرُ إنْ لم يتغيَّر؟؟
*
يا التي جاءَتْ إلى ذاكرتي
من بياضِ الياسمينْ
من سواقي الماء في غر ناطةٍ
ودُمُوع الماندولينْ.
ما الذي يمكنُ أن نفعَلهُ؟
البيانُو غارقٌ في دمعِهِ
والمواني كلُّها مُغْلَقةٌ
ونبيذُ البحر أحمر
ليس عندي للهوى خارطةٌ...
فهو يوماً وردة في عُرْوَتي
وهوَ يوماً في فراش الحُبّ خِنجرْ..
وهْوَ يوماً جَمْرةٌ تُحرقُني
وهْو يوماً في فمي قطَعةُ سُكَّرْ !!
*

Whenever a new love tale
is added to the annals of love
in my hometown,
roses conceive fragrance,
and the crescent of summer
becomes a breast full of milk.

*

For fifty years I've been jumping
from one landmine to another,
preaching to my people
so that they might change.
I haven't demolished the hurdles
of ugliness the way I imagined.
In fact, I've been exploding
in my own fire.
In fifty years I haven't met
a hind that fled her captor,
nor a woman who desired freedom.

*

ُكلّما زَادَتْ أقاصيصُ الهوى
في بلادي قصّةً...
تَحْبَلُ الوردةُ طيباً...
وهلالُ الصيفِ،
يكتظُّ حَليبا!!

*

منذُ خمسَين سَنَهْ
وأنا أقفزُ من لُغْمٍ إلى لُغْمِ
وأدعو أمّتي أن تتغيّرْ
لم أُفَجّرْ حائطَ القُبحِ ، كما خيُّلَ لي
بل أنا كنتُ بناري أتَفجّرْ...
منذُ خمسَين سَنَهْ
لم أُقابلْ ظَبْيَةً تهُربُ من صيّادها...
أو عرفتُ امرأةً راغبة أن تتحرّرْ !!

*

What amazes me
is that every time we meet,
the colour of time in our watches
turns green,
the yearning in our eyes
turns green,
and the moon that rises from your cleavage
turns green.

*

What really amazes me
is the feeling every morning
that whatever I touch or lay eyes on
turns into poetry.
My things and yours – no matter how trivial –
turn into poetry.
The coffee pot – when we are in love –
turns into poetry.
Our favourite poetry books,
the giggle in the cleft of our bathrobes,
the sound of water as it happily courses our backs.

إنَّ ما يُذهلُني
كلّما جئتُ إلى موعدنا
أن لونَ الوقت في سَاعَاتِنا
أصبحَ أحضَرْ...
وبأنَّ البُنَّ في قَهْوَتِنِا
أصبحَ أخضَرْ...
وبأنَّ الشوقَ في أحدا قنا
أصبحَ أخضَرْ...
وبأنَّ القَمَرَ الطالعَ
من رافعة النهدين...
قد أصبح أخضَرْ!!.
*
إنَّ ما يُدهشُني
ذلك الإحساس في كلّ صباحِ
أنَّ ما ألمسُهُ، يصبحُ شِعْرَا...
أنَّ ما أبصرُهُ،يصبحُ شِعْرَا...
أنَّ أشيائي وأشياءَكِ - مهما صَغُرتْ-
تصبحُ شِعرا...
رَكْوَةُ القهوة - في حَالِ الهوى-
تصبحُ شعْرَا...
كُتُبُ الشعر التي تُعجبُنا...
ضحِكةُ البُرْنُس في الحمَّامِ...
صوتُ الماءِ ، ينسابُ على سلْسِلَة
الظَهْر...سعيداً...

Chopin's melodies,
Mozart's symphonies.
The taste of the first kiss before breakfast.
Your white feet diving into the thick carpet,
the brush massaging your hair,
and the eye shadow in the corners of your eyes.
Isn't all of this reason enough
for the entire universe
to transform itself into music and poetry?
All of this, my lady, are pages of history
that will never recur.
That will
never
recur.

*

What has come over me these days, my lady?
Everything I touch,
everything I read,
and everything I write turns green.
My language is green.
The nouns, the verbs, the syntax
and the rhythm of my poetry is green.

*

آلةُ التسجيل...
تنويعاتُ (شُوبَان)
إضاءاتُ (موزارت)...
ومَذاقَ القُبلة الأولى على الريق...
وغَوصُ القَدَم البيضاء في الموكيت...
لَمْسُ الشَعر بالفُرشاةِ...
وضعُ الكُحْل في زاوية العَينيْن...
ماذا يتبقّى
كَيْ يصيرَ الكونُ موسيقى وشِعْرا؟؟.
تلكَ صَفحاتٌ من التاريخ،يا سيِّدتي...
أبداً...لَنْ تتكرَّرْ...
أبداً...لَنْ تتكرَّرْ...
*
مـا الذي ينتابُني في هذه الأيّام،يا سيّدتي؟
كلُّ ما ألمسـهُ،يصبحُ أخضَرْ
كلُّ ما أقرؤه، يصبحُ أخضرْ
كلُّ ما أكتبُهُ، يصبحُ أخضَرْ
لغتي خضراءُ...
والأسماء،والأفعالُ، والهَمزاتُ ، والفتحاتُ،
والضمَّاتُ ، والإيقاع أخضرْ...
وعروض الشِعْر،أخضَرْ...
*

What has mixed the colour in our eyes?
When we talk over the phone,
the sound of our voices turns green.
When we lounge in the living room,
the beads of moisture under your arms turn green.
When we loiter on the sidewalks of sadness,
sadness turns green.
And when we sit in a café,
the waiter, because of your scent, turns green.

*

What's happening to our histories, my lady?
Whenever I squander kisses on your hair,
it grows before my eyes.

*

Oh mystical lady,
you have led me to the springs
and offered me the stars, vineyards, and pines.
Thank you for your gifts,
for I have lived in exile the longest time
until I turned – because of love – green.

ما الذي قد خلَطَ الألوانَ في أعيُننا؟
إن تكلّمنا على الهاتف، صار الصوتُ أخضَرْ..
أو تمدَّدْنا على الديوان
صار القمحُ في إبطَيْكِ أخضَرْ..
أو تسكَّعنا على أرصفةِ الحُزْنِ،
وجدنا أنّ لونَ الحزن أخضرْ..
أو جلسنا مرة، في أيّ مقهى
أصبحَ النادلُ من عطركِ...أخضَرْ!!
*
ما الذي يجري بتاريخي. وتاريخكِ... يا سيّدتي؟
كلّما وزّعتُ قُبلاتي على شَعْركِ...
طالَ الشعْرُ أكثرْ!!
*
آه... يا سيدةَ الماءِ التي تأخُذُني للينابيع....
وتُهديني نُجُوماً...وكروماً...وصُنَوبَرْ...
ألفُ شكرٍ لعطاياكِ، فإنّي
عشْتُ في التيه طويَلاً،
ثمّ أصبحتُ – بفَضْل الحُبّ-أخْضَرْ!! ...

Snow

1996

Snowflakes dance across my windows in London.
They dance over my books, papers, and coffee
cups
as I sit dazzled before this sophisticated talk –
talk I haven't heard for nine months.
I am stunned by this white coup,
this declaration by winter
to overthrow the reactionary summer
and the monotony of green.

*

Snow is the youthful earth
deviating from its theme
and attempting to invent
a new style of writing –
a better mould –
and expressing its infatuation
in a different tongue.

*

لا وسيلةَ للتدفئة سوى أن أحِبَّكِ!

يندُفُ الثلجُ على شبابيكي في لندن
يندُفُ على كُتُبي... وأوراقي...
وفناجِين قَهوَتي
وأنا مبهورٌ بهذا الكلامِ الحَضَاريّ
الذي لم أسمَعْهُ منذ تسعة أشهُرْ..
مَبْهُورٌ بهذا الانقلاب الأبيَضْ
الذي يعلنُهُ الشتاءْ
على رجعيّةِ الصيفْ...
ورَتَابةِ اللونِ الأخضَر..
*
الثلجُ هو حَدَاثةُ الأرضْ
عندما تخرُجُ على النصّ...
وتحاولُ أن تكتبَ بطريقةٍ أخرى
وصياغَةٍ أُخرى
وتُعبّر عن عِشْقِها...
بلغةٍ أُخرى...
*

Me too.
I too want to be wintry,
stormy and unpredictable
in my infatuation.
For I can only be phenomenal
with a phenomenal and mad
lover like you.
I can't be a warrior
in a land
that doesn't bear arms.

*

This snow does not bother me,
nor does the frost.
I resist them
sometimes with poetry,
and sometimes with love,
for there is no other way to keep warm
except by loving you
or writing you a poem.

*

وأنا أيضاً... أُريدُ أن أكونَ في عِشقي..
شتائياً... وانقلابياً... وعاصفاً...
فمع امرأة استثنائية ِمثلكِ
لا يمكنني إلا أن أكون استثنائياً...
ومع عاشقةٍ مجنونةٍ مثلكِ...
لا يمكنني أن أبقى محارباً
على أرض منزوعةِ السلاح!! ...

*

لا يُقلقُني الثلج...
ولا يُزعجني حصارُ الصقيع...
فأنا أُقاومُهُ...
حيناً بالشّعرْ...
وحيناً بالحُبّ...
فليس عندي وسيلةٌ أُخرى للتدفئه...
سوى أن اُحبّكِ...
أو أكتبَ لكِ قصيدةَ حُبّ...

*

With these two magical elements,
I resolve all my sexual hang–ups,
calm all my emotional upheavals,
and melt all my creative blocks.
So don't fret over the weather outside;
real summer lurks within us.

*

I am always capable of
chasing the chill from your hands –
extracting fire from the garnet of your lips –
drawing out from every curve and flowing vessel
within your body
the most exquisite poetry.

*

Oh mistress whose love burns
in my blood like fire,
when you are here with me
there is no need for fireplaces,
hearths or radiators,

بهاتَين الطريقتين السحْريّتينْ...
يمكننَي أن أحلَّ مشاكَلي الجَسَديَّة...
ومشاكلي العاطفيَّة...
ومشاكلي الشعريَّة...
فلا تُشغلي بالكِ بالطّقسِ الخارجيّ
لأنّ الصيَفَ الحَقيقيّ
مَخْبوءٌ في داخِلنا!! ...

*

إنّني قادرٌ دائماً
على استخراجِ الجَمْرِ... من ثلج يَدَيْكِ...
وعلى استخراج النارْ...
من عقيق شفَتيك...
وعلى استخراج الشِعرْ...
من تحت أية رابيةٍ من روابي أنُوثتك...
وأية منطقةٍ حُبْلى بمياهها الجَوْفيَّةَ!!...

*

يا سّيدتي التي يشتعلُ حبُّها في دمي...
كحفْلة ألعابٍ ناريَّة...
حينَ تَكونينَ معي...
فلا فائدةَ من مواقدِ الحَطَبْ
ولا مواقدِ الفحم
ولا مواقدِ الكهرباء

for all the energy sources are contained
within the waves of your oceans,
and all the planets are orbiting
the sun of your breasts.

*

You stand there in your red hood
trembling from your passion,
your voice deflecting off the snow
like so many gold coins.
Don't open your umbrella over my head.
I don't need protection
from doves' feathers or jasmine moons.
I don't want to flee this white siege,
for you and the snow are my companions
on the road to freedom.

*

Oh wintry being, I adore you.
Don't let go of my hand
and don't fear the angora wool
of my childish fantasies.

فمصادرُ الطاقة كلُّها
موجودةٌ في أمواج بحاركْ...
والكواكبُ كلُّها...
تدورُ حول شمس نهديكِ!!...
*
يا ذاتَ القُبَّعةِ الحمراء...
التي ترتجفُ من شدّة العشق...
يا التي يسقُطُ صوتُهاَ على الثلج كليرة ذهبيَّة...
لا تفتحي المظلّة فوق رأسي
فأنا لا أريد الحمايةَ من زَغب الحَمامْ...
ونُثَاراتِ القُطنْ
وأقمار الياسمينْ...
لا أريدُ الهُروبَ من هذا الحصار الأبيضْ...
فأنتِ... والثلجْ...
صديقايَ على دُرُوب الحريّة...
*
أيّتُها الشتائيَّةُ التي أُحبُّها...
لا تشيلي يدكِ من يدي...
ولا تخافي على صوُفِ الأنغُورا...
من نَزَواتي الطُفُوليَّه...

How often I desired
to write a poem in snow,
make love in snow
and explore the possibilities
of feeling love's fever in snow.

*

Why are you shivering, woman,
like a terrified squirrel
through the jungle of my chest?
All the men in the world loved their women
in the month of July.
All the love epics were written
in the month of July.
All the revolutions in the name of freedom
took place in the month of July.
Allow me to violate the summer norm:
Allow me to sleep with you
for only one night
on a pillow woven from silver
and snow flakes.

فلطالما تمنيتُ...
أن أكتبَ قصيدةً فوق الثلجْ...
وأُحبَّ امرأةً فوق الثلجْ...
وأُجَرِّبَ كيف يمكنُ لعاشقٍ
أن يحترقَ بنار الثلج!!...

*

يا سيّدتي التي تقفزُ كسَنجَابةٍ خائفةٍ
على أشجار صدري...
كلُّ عشّاقِ العالم أحبُّوا حبيباتِهم
في شهر تَمُّوزْ...
وكلُّ ملاحم العشق
كُتَبتْ في شهر تَمُّوزْ...
وكَلُّ الثوراتِ من أجل الحرِّيّةْ...
وقَعَتْ في شهر تَمُّوزْ...
فاسْمَحي لي...
أن أخرج على هذا التوقيت الصيفيّ...
وأنام معكِ... ليلةً واحدَةً...
على مخدّة من خيطان الفَضّة...
والثَلجِ المندُوفْ...

Daily Love Exercises

1996

I don't have anything more to tell you
in the new year,
except that I love you with all the instinct
of a voracious fish,
and that I will continue my exercises in passion
until I become the first Arabian stallion
to reach the zenith of your breasts
and the first swimmer to cross the sea of femininity
from coast to coast.

*

For a millennium before history
to a millennium after,
I have been practising the sport of love.
I inhale deeply,
exhale,
massage my body with violet oil
and jump from the precipice
of your right breast
to the precipice of your left

تمريناتُ يوميَّةُ على الحُبّ!!

ليس عندي ما أقولُهُ لكِ في العام الجديد
سوى أنني أحبُّكِ...
بكلِّ غريزة الأسماك المتوحشّةْ...
وأنني سوف أواصلُ تمريناتي على العِشقْ...
حتى أكونَ أوَّلَ حصانٍ عربيْ
يصلُ إلى قِمّة نَهْدَيْكِ...
وأوّلَ سابحٍ يقطعُ المحيطَ الأنثَويْ
من الماءِ... إلى الماء...

*

منذُ مليون سَنَةٍ قبلَ التاريخْ
إلى مليون سنةٍ بعدَ التاريخْ
وأنا أتمرَّنُ على رياضة الحُبْ...
أسْتَنْشقُ بعُمقْ
وأزفرُ بَعُمقْ...
وأدلّكُ جَسَدي بزيْت البنفسَجْ...
وأقفزُ من شُرفْةِ نهدَكِ الأيَمنْ...
إلى شُرفة نهدكِ الأيسرْ...

so that I may retain my physical stamina,
sentimental vigour, poetic inspiration
and be worthy of becoming an emerald ring
that flashes on your finger
or a slender Spanish earring
that dangles in your hair.

*

From the moment
I first breathed the scent of femininity,
I've been practising passion non–stop.
Practising like
an opera singer in front of a mirror,
an actor memorising his script,
a maestro rehearsing his orchestra.
I did not believe in spontaneity or improvisation,
either in love or in poetry.
I always sought a new language
to dazzle you with its rhythm,
a new poetry to seduce you with its silky words.

*

حتى أظلَّ محتَفظاً بلياقتي الجسديّة...
والعاطفيّةِ... والشعّريةْ...
وأكون جديراً بأن أكونَ خاتماً من الزمرُّدْ
يلمعُ في اصبعكْ...
أو قُرْطاً أسبانيا طويلاً...
يتدلَّى من أُذُنيْكِ...

*

منذُ أنْ شَمَمْتُ رائحةَ الأُنوثَةْ...
وأنا أتمرَّنُ على أعمال العِشقْ
بدون توقّفْ
كما يتمرَّن مُغنّي الأوبرا أمامَ المرآةْ
والمّمثلُ على قراءة النصّ المسرحي
وراقصُ الباليه على رسْم خَطَواتهْ
وقائدُ الأوركسترا على إدارة العَازفينْ
لم أكُنْ أؤمنُ بالفوضى والارتجالْ
لا في الحُبّ .. ولا في الشِعر..
كنتُ أبحث دائماً...
عن لغةٍ جديدةٍ تَنْبَهرينَ بإيقاعاتها
وعن قصيدةٍ جديدةْ...
تنامينَ على حرير كلماتها
وعن قُبْلةٍ استثنائيّةْ...
تُغَيّرُ تاريخَ شفَتَيْكِ!!

*

Since I was a babe in my mother's womb
I've had designs on you.
And until I became proficient
in painting with words,
I've had to fight my tribe
for permission to stroll with you
down the road of civilisation.

*

I don't want to love you
in the conventional way
or shatter my feelings in front of you
in the conventional way.
I want to fine–tune you
the way I fine–tune my poems,
design your breasts
in the Andalusian architectural style,
the Roman,
the Byzantine,
or the Pharaohs' styles,

منذُ أن كنتُ في بَطْن أُمّي
وأنا أخطّطُ حتى تكوني حبيبتي...
ومنذُ أن احترفتُ الرَسْمَ بالكلمات...
وأنا أقاتلُ عشيرتي...
حتّى تسمحَ أن أتمشّى معكِ قليلاً
في شارع الحَضَارَةْ!!

*

لا أريدُ أن أُحبَّكِ... كيفما اتّفَقْ...
وأُبعثرَ أحاسيسي أمَامَكِ...
كيفما اتّفق...
أريدُ أن أُدَوْزِنَك كما أُدَوْزِنُ شِعْري
وأهَنْدسَ صَدْرَكَ...
على طريقة العَمارة الأندلسيّةْ
أو الرومانيَّةْ...
أو البيزَنطيَّةْ...
أو الفرعُونيّةْ...

make each dome among your domes,
each vault within your vaults,
each piece of your mosaic
and each pyramid amidst your pyramids
an historical monument.

*

In each love story I begin,
I strive to emulate the traditions of gallantry,
the purity of pedigrees,
the chivalry of Arabian steeds,
and attend you like a painter his canvas,
the musician his etude,
the sculptor his clay,
and the sparrow his stream.

*

I have been practising
around the clock
how to journey to the moon
and discover countries of jasmine.
I was preparing myself
to be a great lover,
marching under the Arch of Triumph
with a red carpet under my feet

وأجعلَ كلَّ قبّةٍ من قبَابكْ...
وكلَّ قَوْسٍ من أقواسَكْ...
وكلَّ قطعةٍ من فُسَيْفُسَائِك...
وكلَّ هَرَمٍ من أهراماتِكْ...
مَعْلَماً من معالم التارَيخ!!
*
في كُلِّ قصّة حُبٍ أدخُلُها...
أبقى ملتزماً َبتقاليد الصهيلْ...
ونَقَاءِ
السُلالاتْ...
ومُروءات الخيل العربيّةْ...
وأتعامَلُ معك...
كما يتعاملُ الَرسَّامُ مع لوحتِهْ
والموسيقىُّ مع معزوفتهْ...
والنَّحاتُ مع مَنْحوتتْهَ...
والعُصْفورُ مع جدولِ ماءْ...
*
على مدى أربعٍ وعشرينَ ساعَةْ
كنتُ أتمرَّنْ على الهبوط على أرضِ القَمَرْ
واكتشاف بلاد الياسمينْ...
كنتُ أهَيِّءُ نفسي
كي أكون عاشقاً كبيراً...
يمرُّ من تحتِ قَوْسِ النصرْ
ويُفْرَشُ تحتَ قَدَميْهَ السجَّادُ الأحمَرْ..

and a flock of doves flying over my parade.
I wanted to be superior
in my love letters,
not just a starving lover
begging on the sidewalk of love
or stumbling like an idiot in front of women.

*

I am dedicated
to your love full–time
on Saturdays and Sundays,
Thursdays and Fridays,
and even on Eids and holidays –
for you are very beautiful
and there is so little time.
And I work like an industrious ant
mornings and evenings,
summer and winter,
autumn and spring,
just so I can bring you
a bottle of Arabian eye shadow
to darken your eyes,
and weave for you
a pillow of cashmere wool
to rest on.

*

وتطيرُ فوق موكبه أسرابُ الحَمَامْ
كنتُ أريدُ أن أكونَ متفوّقاً
في خطابي الغراميِّ
لا مُجَّردَ عاشقٍ درويشْ...
يتسوَّلُ على أرصفة الحبْ
ويَتَلعْثَمُ كمجذُوبٍ أمَامِ النساءْ!!
*
أنني مُتفرّغٌ لحبّكِ... يا سيّدتي.
فلا سَبْتَ... ولا أحدْ...
ولا خميسَ... ولا جُمُعَةْ...
ولا أعيادَ... ولا إجازات...
فأنتِ جميلةٌ جداً...
والوقَتُ ضيّقٌ جداً...
وأنا أشتغلُ كالنَمْلةِ المجتهدَةْ
صبَاحاً... ومساءً...
صيَفاً... وشتاءً...
خريفاً... وربيعاً...
حتّى أجلبَ لكِ قارورةً من العطر الحجازيْ...
تتكحّلينَ بها...
وأغزلَ لكِ وسادةً من صُوف الكَشْميرْ...
تنامينَ عليها!!
*

I exercise every day
to satisfy your femininity,
so that the electric current remains humming
through the vessels of your body.
At the break of dawn,
I breathe hot air into your left ear
to wake you up.
Midmorning,
I blow dry your hair
as if you were a girl on her way to school.
At noon,
I draw, using red wine,
a crescent on your back.
In the afternoon,
I hide a pigeon under your blue satin blouse,
and at midnight,
I don't know how to seduce you,
so I write a verse of poetry
in the hollow of your belly.

*

I always want to be right here,
a bee licking the honey from your toes,
buzzing with the joy of my employment.

*

إنّني أتمَّرنُ كلَّ يومْ..
كي أُرضي أنوثَتك..
وحتى يظلّ التَّيارُ آلكهربائيْ
مُتواصلاً في أسلاك جَسَدِكْ
ففي غَبَش الفجرْ
أنفُخُ في أُذُنك اليسرى، حتى تَسْتَيْقظِي...
وفي وقت الضَحُى
أَنشَفُ شَعرَكِ بمُجفّف الشَعْرْ..
كطفلةٍ ذاهبةٍ إلى المدرسَةْ...
وعند الظهيرةْ
أرسُمُ بالنبيذ الأحمرْ
هلالاً على ظَهْرِكْ...
وفي وقت القيلُوَلَةْ
أخبئُ حَمَامَةْ..
تحتَ قميص السَاتَان الأزرق..
وفي منتصفِ الليلْ..
لا أعرفُ كيف أتحرَّشُ بكْ..
فأكتُبُ بيتاً من الشّعرْ..
على سيراميكِ خاصرتِكْ!!

*

أُريدُ أن أظلَّ دائماً
نَحْلةً تلحسُ العَسَل عن أصابع قدَمْيكِ
حتى لا أبقى عاطلاً عن العَمَلْ!!

*

After fifty years
of primary, secondary, and higher education,
I remain an apprentice at the art of loving a woman –
how to care for the shape of her hand,
the sheen of her breasts.
And I am still studying how to protect her.
Since freedom has no ceiling
and democracy no ceiling,
so then is our knowledge of women.

*

After fifty years
I still labour in the workshop of love
with great enthusiasm.
And I still laugh at all the men
who graduated from the University of Love
in my country
without seeing the thigh of a woman
except on TV screens.

بعدَ خمسينَ عاماً..
من التحصيل الابتدائيِّ، والمتوسّطِ، والعالي..
لا زلتُ أتعلَّمُ كيفَ أُحبّ امرأةْ..
وكيف أعتني بشَمْعِ يَدَيْها..
وفضَّةِ نهدَيْها...
وكيف أخافُ عليها...
فكما أن الحرّيةَ لا سَقْفَ لها...
والديمقراطيةَ لا سقفَ لها..
فإن المعارفَ النسائيَّةْ...
لا سَقْفَ لها!!
*
بعد خمسينَ عاماً
لا زلتُ أعملُ في وَرْشَةِ الحُبِّ... بحمَاسٍ عظيمْ
ولا زلتُ أضحكُ من جميع الذين تخرَّجُوا
من جامعات الحُبّ... في بلادنا...
وهُمْ لم يُشاهدُوا فَخْذَ امرأةْ...
إلا على شاشَة التلفزيونْ!!...

Does He Think?

1961

Does he think
that I'm a toy,
that he can play with me
however and whenever he likes?
I wouldn't even consider
going back to him!
And he comes today
as if nothing had happened,
playing innocent like a child.
He's come back to say
that we were meant for each other,
that I'm his one and only love.
And he brought flowers!
How could I turn him away
when he brought flowers
and the line of his lips
read like the history of my love?
I can hardly recall how quickly
I sought sanctuary in his arms,
how, despite my boiling anger,

أيَظُنُّ ؟

أيظنُّ أنّي لُعْبَةٌ بيديهِ ؟
أنا لا أُفكِّرُ في الرجوعِ إليهِ
اليومَ عادَ . كأنَّ شيئاً لم يكُنْ
وبراءةُ الأطفالِ في عَيْنَيْـــهِ
ليقولَ لي : إنّي رفيقةُ دربهِ
وبأنّني الحبُّ الوحيــدُ لَدَيْهِ
حَمَلَ الزهورَ إليَّ .. كيف أرُدُّهُ
وصِبَايَ مرسومٌ على شَفَتَيْهِ
ما عدتُ أذكرُ .. والحرائقُ في دمي
كيفَ التجأتُ أنا إلى زَنْدَيهِ

I hid my head in his body
as if I were a long–lost child
reuniting with her parents.
Even my discarded dresses were happy
and danced at his feet.
I forgave him instantly
and asked how he was.
I wept endlessly
and without realising it,
left my hand to sleep
like an exhausted sparrow in his,
and instantly my spite melted away.
Who was it who said
I felt spite for him?
How adamant I was!
I wasn't going back to him,
yet I did.
And how sweet is my homecoming!

خبَّأتُ رأسي عندهُ .. وكأنَّني
طفلٌ أعادوهُ إلى أبَوَيْهِ
حتى فساتيني التي أهملتُها
فرحتْ بهِ .. رَقَصَتْ على قَدَمَيْهِ
سامحتُهُ .. وسألتُ عن أخبارهِ
وبكيتُ ساعاتٍ على كَتِفَيْهِ
وبدون أنْ أدري تركتُ له يدي
لتنامَ كالعصفور بينَ يديْهِ ..
ونسيتُ حقدي كُلَّهُ في لحظةٍ
مَنْ قالَ إنّي قد حقدتُ عليهِ
كم قلتُ إنّي غيرُ عائدةٍ لهُ
ورجعتُ .. ما أحلى الرجوعَ إليهِ .

My Angry Cat

1961

You're repeating yourself
for the twentieth time.
Is there another man in my life?
Yes. Yes. What did you think?
Even graveyards have visitors.
There are, my dear sir,
a lot of men out there,
and no garden is ever devoid of birds.
You're just an experience I had,
and here I am,
tired and bored from this experience,
out from under your spell.
I'm cured of all
my weakness and gullibility.
Niceties do, after all, always end.
You love me!
There you go again,
dredging up all that ancient history.
And since when did you ever show
the slightest interest in me
outside the contour of my hips?
Where does this sudden gush of love come from?

قِطّتي الغَضْبَى

للمرّة العشرين .. كررْتَهَا
"هل في حياتي رَجُلٌ آخَرُ؟"
نَعَمْ ..نَعَمْ..فهلْ تصوّرتَني
مقبرةً ليسَ لها زائرُ
ما أكثرَ الرجالَ .. يا سّيدي
لا روضةٌ إلا لها طائرُ
تجربةً كانتْ .. و ها أنّني
نَجَوْتُ من سحركَ يا ساحرُ
شُفيتُ من ضعفي ومن طيبتي
فطيبةُ النفس لها آخِـــرُ
تُحبُّني ! ليتَكَ ما قلتَها
هذا حديثٌ غابِرٌ .. غابرُ
منذُ متى ؟ أصبحتَ تَهْتَمُّ بي
منذُ متى هذا الهوى الغامرُ ؟

I was never anything more
than a forsaken chair
among your expensive furniture,
a garden you chose to raze
without shame or repentance.
Why are you staring at my breasts
as if you owned them?
And why do you weep as if you
stood before a lost kingdom?
Your glorious kingdom, dear sir,
has just crumbled.
There. I've settled my score
in an instant.
You tell me now
who's losing the game.
I opened myself to you
like the Garden of Eden,
gave you all the sweet fruit
and green grass you desired.

هل كنتُ إلا مقعداً مُهْمَلاً
يضمُّهُ أثاثُكَ الفاخـــرُ ؟
مزرعةً نَهَبْتَ خَيْرَاتِها
لا ذمَّةٌ تنهى ولا زاجـــرُ
ترنو إلى مفاتني مثلما
يرنو إلى أمواله التاجرُ
يا أيُّها الباكي على مُلْكِهِ
لقد تداعى مُلْكُكَ الزاهرُ
حسابيَ القديمُ .. صفَّيْتُهُ
بلحظةٍ . فمنْ بنا الخاسرُ ؟
كانَتْ لكَ الجنَّاتُ مفتوحةً
ثمارُها ، وعُشْبُها الناضرُ

Today I offer you
neither heaven nor hell.
This is what you get
for acting the ungrateful.
You faithless. If you'd only treated me
like a human being –just once –
this other man wouldn't exist.

واليومَ .. لا نــــارٌ ولا جنَّةٌ
هذا جزاءُ الكُفْرِ يا كافِرُ
لو كُنْتَ إنساناً معي مــرةً
ما كانَ هذا الرجلُ الآخَرُ !

Words

1961

He speaks to me, while we dance,
with mellifluous words.
With his words, he lifts me from the dance floor
and plants me in a cloud.
Black rain drizzles my eyes
as I sail into the pink night.
I am a small girl curled in the cup of his hand.
He offers me seven moons
and a bouquet of songs.
He gifts me the sun,
the summer, and a flock of swallows.
He tells me that I am a masterpiece,
that my worth is that of a thousand stars.
I am a treasure, he whispers,
the most beautiful painting he has ever seen.
He speaks words that dazzle me,
that make me forget my feet and the dance floor.

كَلِمآت

يسْمِعُني .. حين يُراقصُني
كَلِمَاتٍ .. ليستْ كالكَلِماتْ
يأخذني من تحت ذراعي
يزرَعُني في إحدى الغَيْمَاتْ
والمَطَرُ الأسودُ في عَيْني
يتساقطُ زخّاتٍ .. زَخّاتْ
يَحْمِلُني معهُ .. يَحْمِلُني
لمساءٍ ورديّ الشُرُفَاتْ
وأنا كالطفلة في يدِهِ
كالريشةِ تحملُها النَسَماتْ
يحملُ لي سَبْعَةَ أقمارٍ
بيديهِ .. وحُزْمةَ أُغنيّاتْ
يُهْديني شمساً .. يُهْديني
صيفاً .. وقطيعَ سُنُونُوّاتْ
يُخبرني أنّي تُحْفَتُهُ
وأساوي آلافَ النَجْماتْ
وبأنّي كنزٌ .. وبأنّي
أجملُ ما شاهدَ من لوحاتْ
يروي أشياءَ .. تدوّخُني
تنسيني المرقصَ والخَطَواتْ

He speaks words that contradict my history,
that, instantly, make a woman out of me.
With his words he builds me a palace
in which I reside a few blissful moments –
only to return to my table
with nothing but words.

َكلِمَاتٍ .. تقلبُ تاريخي
تجعلني امرأةً .. في لَحَظَاتْ
يبني لي قَصْراً من وَهْم
لا أسكُنُ فيه سوى لَحَظَاتْ
وأعودُ .. أعودُ لطاولتي
لا شيءَ معي .. إلاَّ كَلِمَاتْ

The Play

1961

I declare in public
that you are not my love,
while deep in my heart
I know I am a liar.
I claim nothing exists between us
to spare us grief.
I deny the rumours of love
despite their sweetness.
I turn my happy story into emptiness.
I assert in vain my indifference.
I suffocate my yearning.
I don the robes of a monk
and flee from the heavens in your eyes.
Oh my love,
I play the role of the fool
and fail miserably in my act.
For neither the night
can conceal the stars,
nor can the sea
its drifting vessels.

التمثيليّة

أقولُ أمامَ الناسِ : لستِ حَبيبتي
وأعْرِفُ في الأعماقِ كَمْ كنتُ كاذِبا
وأزْعَمُ أنْ لا شئَ يَجْمَعُ بينَنا
لأُبْعِدَ عَنْ نَفْسي وَعَنْكِ المتاعِبا
وأنْفِي إشاعاتِ الهَوَى، وهْيَ حُلْوَةٌ
وأجْعَلُ تاريخي الجميلَ خَرائِبا
وأعْلِنُ في شكْلِ غَبِيٍّ بَراءَتي
وأذْبَحُ شَهْواتي، وأُصبحُ راهِبا
وأقْتُلُ عِطْري عامِداً مُتَعَمِّداً
وأخْرُجُ من جنّاتِ عَيْنَيْكِ هاربا
أقومُ بِدَوْرٍ مُضْحِكٍ، يا حبيبَتي
وأرْجعُ منْ تَمْثيلِ دوريَ خائِبا
فلا اللّيلُ يُخْفي، لو أرادَ، نُجومَهُ
ولا البَحْرُ يُخفي، لو أرادَ، المراكِبا

Only With Me

1961

You will always remember my fingers.
If you were to live a thousand years,
you would always, my dear, remember my
fingers.
So sleep with whomever you desire.
Make love in the streets if you want.
Sleep with the taxi driver, with the homosexual,
with the cobbler or the farmer.
Sleep with the kings or with the thieves,
or even, if it's what you desire,
the monks in their monasteries.
It makes no difference if you
sleep with women, the wind, or hurricanes,
you'll only feel like a natural woman with me.

إلاّ مَعي

ستذكرينَ دائماً أصابعي ..
لو ألفَ عامٍ عِشْتِ .. يا عزيزتي
ستذكرينَ دائماً أصابعي ..
فضاجِعي مَنْ شئتِ أن تُضاجعي ..
ومارسي الحُبَّ.. على أرصفةِ الشوارع
نامي مع الحوذيِّ ، واللوطيِّ ،
والإسكافي .. والُمزَارع ..
نامي مع الملوكِ ، واللصوص ،
والنُسَّاكِ في الصَّوامع ..
نامي مع النساءِ – لا فرقَ–
مع الريح ، مع الزوابع ..
فلن تكوني امرأةً ..
إلاَّ معي .. إلاَّ معي ...

The Evil Poem

1956

Amidst the drenching rains
and the howling October winds,
she's stretching alongside her girlfriend.
The door squeaks as it opens
and the key twists in wild abandon.
There's something going on between them
and only two know it – the lamp and me –
a love story that's better left untold,
for love perishes when described explicitly.
The room becomes a mess as they remove their
jewelry
and fine silk clothes.
Buttons stealthily flee their holes,
for the night is revealing:
A she–wolf breast–feeds her she–wolf.
As a hand reaches further beyond,
further down,
the bed cover takes flight as one pulls
and the other lets go.

القصِيَدة الِشّرِيَرة

مَطَرٌ .. مَطَرٌ .. وصديقتُها
معها ، ولتشرينَ نواحُ
والبابُ تئنُّ مفاصلُهُ
ويعربدُ فيه المفتاحُ
شيءٌ بينهما .. يعرفُهُ
إثنان ، أنا والمصباحُ
وحكايةُ حبّ ٍ.. لا تُحكى
في الحبّ ، يموتُ الإيضاحُ
الحجرةُ فوضى .. فحُليٌّ
تُرْمى .. وحريرٌ ينزاحُ
ويغادرُ زرٌّ عروتَهُ
بفتورٍ ، فالليلُ صباحُ
الذئبةُ تُرضع ذئبتَها
ويدٌ تجتاحُ وتجتاحُ
ودثارٌ فرَّ .. فواحدةٌ
تُدنيه ، وأخرى ترتاحُ

Four breasts talk face to face,
whispering words that freely flow.

*

They're like two doves in the park,
playfully pecking and gently stroking
with their beaks and feathers.
The beads of their necklaces break loose,
and tender skin is scraped raw
by razor–sharp nails in the darkness.
Suddenly, the sighing turns to barking.
A breast ceases its courtship
and rages for the wounds it suffered.
Death is vanquished,
and the lamp slumps back from exhaustion.

*

Oh, sister, please please don't panic.
I will always be here for you.
Seek refuge in my bosom and hide behind my wings.
Do you think I have been created Woman
so that her breasts are chewed by ghouls?
Is it abnormal, sister, for an apple to kiss an apple?
We are but two women – who like all women
have their climaxes, sighs and gusts.

وحوارُ نهودٍ أربعةٍ
تتهامسُ ، والهمس مباحُ
*
كطيورٍ بيضٍ في روضٍ
تتناقرُ .. والريشُ سلاحُ
حَبَّاتُ العِقْدَيَنِ انفرطتْ
من لهوٍ ، وانهدَّ وشاحُ
فاللحمُ الطفلُ ، يخدِّشهُ
في العتمة ، ظِفْرٌ سفاّحُ
وجُزازةُ شعرٍ .. وانقطعتْ
فالصوتُ المهموسُ نباحُ
ويكسِّرُ نهدٌ واقعَهُ
ويثورُ ، فللجرحِ جراحُ
ويموتُ الموتُ .. ويستلقي
ممَّا عاناهُ المصباحُ ..
*
يا أختيَ ، لا .. لا تضطربي
إنيّ لكِ صدرٌ وجناحُ
أتراني كُوِّنتُ امرأةً
كي تمضغَ نهدي الأشباحُ
أشذوذٌ .. أختاهُ إذا ما
لَثمَ التفّاحَ التفاحُ
نحنُ امرأتان .. لنا قِمَمٌ
ولنا أنواءٌ .. ورياحُ

A Very Realistic Poem

1995

I've known women here and there,
a pretty face here
and a slender waist there.
I've serenaded in every country,
but I never declared
to any woman who rendezvoused with me
or to any woman with whom I had a casual affair,
"I love you forever."
There is no "forever" in the language of love,
for all beautiful women come one day
and leave in another,
and only God stays forever.

*

I write poetry for the sake of poetry.
I don't seek admiration
or blend poetry with infatuation
and sex with songs.
I do not haggle on the price of my words,
for my most precious possessions are words.

قصيدةٌ واقعيّةٌ جدّاً...

عَرَفتُ نساءً هُنا.. ونساءً هناكْ..
ووجهاً جميلاً هُنا..
وقواماً رشيقاً هناكْ..
وغنّيتُ أحلى القَصَائدِ تحتَ نوافذِ كُلِّ بَلَدْ..
ولكنني لم أقُلْ مرةً
لأية سيّدة جالَستَنْي
وأيَّة عابرةٍ صافَحَتْني
"أحبُّكِ حتى الأبدْ"
فليسَ هَنالكَ في لُغَةِ العشْقِ
شيءٌ يُسمَّى (الأَبَدْ)...
فكلُ الجميلاتِ يأتينَ يوماً
ويَرْحَلنَ يوماً
ويبقى الوحيدُ الأحَدْ...

*

أنا أكتُبُ الشعرَ للشِعر..
لا للوصول إلى جَنَّة المُعْجَبَاتْ
ولا أخلُطُ الشعرَ بالعشْقِ،
والجنْسَ بالأغْنياتْ
ولستُ أساومُ يوماً على كَلمَاتي..
فأقْدَسُ مُقْتَنَياتي هي الكَلماتْ...

If you were to be the city of my love,
the poem will stay the capital of pride.

*

I could be soft and sweet,
but I could never allow myself
to blackmail the beautiful and gullible,
and I don't let myself assassinate diction
and slaughter the expressions and the alphabet,
for my heart pounds, when I love,
in a linguistic chest.

*

I might be in love with you,
but I won't be dragged into faking words,
and I won't amuse myself with bribing your
breast,
day in, day out.
I am a man who wouldn't spill the blood of
jasmine
or violate the pride of precious stone.

*

إذا كنتِ أنتِ.. مدينةَ حُبّي
ستبقى القصيدةُ عاصمةَ الكبرياءْ...
*
أنا قد أكونُ رقيقاً، وعَذْباً
ولكنني لا أُبيحُ لنفسي
ابتزازَ الجميلاتِ والساذَجاتْ..
ولستُ أبيحُ لنفسي اغتيالَ اللُّغَهْ،
وذَبْحَ التعابير والمفرداتْ
فقلبي، إذا ما عَشِقْتُ، يدَقُّ بصدْر اللُّغاتْ...
*
أنا قد أكونُ أُحبُّكِ..
لكنّني لا أُوَرّطُ نَفسي بتَنْميق أي كلامْ
ولا أتسلّى برَشْوة نَهدَيْك..
عند الصباح وعند المساءْ
أنا رَجُلٌ لا يُريقُ دَمَ الياسمينْ..
ولا يَتعدّى على كبرياء الرّخَامْ...
*

I won't lose my head
if confronted with the chalices of beauty,
and I won't lose my step
or make the mistake of divulging what's taboo,
I know how to keep a safe distance
between my poems and the love bed.

*

I don't drown, when in love,
in an inch of water.
I don't speak fancy or intellectualise
or boast my feathers like a rooster when we meet.
And I don't lurk like a wolf among the deer.
I don't cheat when I play my hand in love,
and I can't write in air.

*

I don't play the role of the lover
behind closed curtains,
for your love is not a figure of speech or a
metaphor,
but a foundation stone of a civilisation.

*

أنا لا أضيّعُ راسـي
أمامَ كُؤوس الجَمالْ
ولا أترنح ذاتَ اليمين، وذاتَ الشمالْ
ولا أتورّطُ في قول ما لا يُقالْ
وأعرفُ كيف أقيسُ المسافةَ..
بين قصائدِ شعري
وبين سرير الوَصَالْ!!

*

أنا لستُ أغرقُ، حينَ أحبُّكِ،
في شبْرِ ماءْ..
ولا أتفَاصَحُ. لا أتَثاقَفُ
لا أتجمَّلُ كالديك في لحظات اللقاءْ..
ولا أتَمَسْكنُ كالذَئب بين الظَباءْ..
أنا لا أغشُّ بأوراق حُبّي
ولا أستطيعُ الكتابةَ فوقَ الهَواءْ...

*

أنا لا أمثّلُ دورَ العشيق..
وراء الستَارَهْ..
فحبكِ ليسَ مجازاً وليس استعارهْ..
ولكنه حجرٌ في أساس الحضارهْ..

*

I don't say that I will stem the full moon
from your eyes,
and I don't claim that I will harvest the fruit
from your lips.
I don't claim that my love will change the course
of fate and destiny,
so don't be alarmed if I behave strangely,
for I am just a poet who enjoys snapping photos.

*

I am a poet who still has on his lips
drops of his mother's milk.
So don't listen to the hearsay of the tribesmen,
for I have rebelled against them
since I was in my mother's womb.

*

أنا لا أقولُ بأنّي
سأطْلعُ من ناظريكِ القَمرْ
ولا أدّعي أنني سوف أُسْقِطُ من شَفتيْكِ الثَمَرْ..
ولا أدّعي أن حُبي
يُغيّرُ مَجْرَى القَضاءِ.. ومَجرَى القَدَرْ..
فلا تَقْلَقي من سلُوكَي الغريبْ
أنا شاعر يَتسلّى بأخذِ الصُوَرْ!!
*
أنا شاعرٌ لا يزالُ على شَفَتْيهِ
حَليبُ الطُفُولَهْ..
فلا تسمعي ما يقولُ رجالُ القبيلةِ عنّي
فإني مُذْ كنتُ في بطنِ أمي
رفضتُ قرارَ القبيلهْ!!
*

I don't babble on when I am severely in love,
and I don't claim that I moved mountains
or split the seas for you.
My silence suffices;
my fingers transform into birds,
and my silence becomes silk.

*

I might die of lust and love,
but I wouldn't trade poetry for pretty eyes,
a slender waist,
or a breast laden with goodies,
for the poem is my life's fairest lady.
And after I've declared my confession,
would women forgive me?

أنا لا أُثَرْثِرُ..
حين أكونُ بحالة عشقٍ.. كثيرا..
ولا أدّعي أنني قد نَقلتُ الجبالَ
لأجلكِ أنتِ.. وأني شَقَقْتُ البُحُورا..
ولكنني أكتفي بُسكوتي
فتغدو أصابعُ كفي طُيورا..
ويُصبحُ صمَتي حريرا..
*
أنا قد أموتُ اشتْهاءً وعشقاً
ولكنني لا أُقايضُ شِعْري
بطرفٍ كحيلٍ..
وخَصْرٍ نحيل..
ونهدٍ يُخّبئُ لي الطيِّباتْ
فإنَّ القصيدةَ أجملُ سيّدةٍ في حياتي
فهل بعدَ نشرْ اعترافي
تُسامحني السيّداتْ؟؟

The Last Declaration Of King Schariar

1996

Use your head, my lady.
What you say about another woman
in the drawers of my memory
is fiction
and figments of your imagination.
You are the first,
and the rest of earthly women
are mere grains of sand.

*

Don't worry.
Don't worry.
There isn't a woman,
either fair, tan,
black or yellow,
who attracts my attention.
I don't dance, while in love,
fifty tight ropes,
or sing a thousand tunes.
So rest easy, sweetheart.

البيانُ الأخير... من الملِكِ شَهْرَيارْ !!

كَبِّري عَقْلَكِ، يا سيِّدتي
إنَّ ما تحكيَنهُ عن وُجُود امرأةٍ ثانيةٍ...
في جَوَاريري... وفي ذاكَرتي
هو تأليفٌ روائيٌّ... وشَطْحَاتُ خيالِ
إنَّكِ الأولى...
وما يتبقّى من نساءِ الأرض...
ذَرَّاتُ رِمَالِ...

*

لا تَخَافي...
لا تَخَافي...
ما هناكَ امرأةٌ شقراءُ... أو سمراءُ...
أو سوداءُ... أو صفراءُ...
تَستْدَعي اهتمامي
أنا لا أرقُصُ في الحُبِّ
على خمسينَ حَبْلاً...
لا ولا أشدُو على ألفِ مَقَامِ...
إنّني أؤمنُ بالتوحيد في دين الهوى
فَضَعي رِجْلَيْكِ في الثلجِ...
ونامي...

Now who would that other woman be,
and what would she look like?
There are beauties on every sidewalk,
but only your face emerges from the crowd.
Fashion models arouse emotions in mirrors,
only I would never embrace a synthetic breast.
Famous starlets sign autographs left and right,
yet I see none before me.

*

The Nizarism era no longer exists.
All my skirmishes
and romantic conquests have fizzled out.
I no longer possess in my tents
a single sabre,
a single steed,
or a single gold bracelet.
So stop agonising, my lady.
I don't have a second front to conquer,
for I have become a member of the party of peace!

*

Rest easy, sweetheart.
There is no woman who can rob you of your
throne,

مَنْ تكونُ المرأةُ الأخرى...؟
وما أوصافُها؟
الجميلاتُ على كلِّ رصيفٍ...
غيرَ أنَي لا أرى غيرَكِ في هذا الزحَامِ...
والموديلاتُ يُحرّكْنَ أحَاسيسَ المرايا...
غيرِ أنّي لم أُعانقْ في حياتي
أيَّ نَهْدٍ من رخَامِ...
والشهيراتُ يُوزّعن التواقيعَ يميناً...
وشمالاً...
غير أنيَ لا أرى شيئاً أمامي...
*
انتهى العصرُ النزاريُّ... الذي أسّسْتُهُ
وانتهت كلُّ حُرُوبي...
وفُتُوحاتِ غرامي...
لم أعُدْ أمَلكُ سيفاً واحداً...
أو حصاناً واحداً...
أو سواراً ذهبّياً واحداً تحتَ الخيَامِ...
فاستريحي من عَذَاباتكِ، يا سيّدَتي
ليس عندي جَبْهَةٌ ثانيةٌ أفتحُها...
بعدما أصبحتُ من حِزْب السلامِ!!
*
إطْمئنّي...
ما هناكَ امرأةٌ تسرقُ منكِ العَرْشَ، يا سيِّدتي

for I know my way to the dovecotes very well,
and I know who breast–fed me with passion
and taught me the sweetest talk.
So tell me:
How can I possibly flee from my mother's breast
and from the berries that ooze from her nipples?
and from the sun that blazes when she laughs?
Tell me, my one and only,
how I can reject the breast
that fed me sugarcane, mango and Syrian
citronella?
And how can I possibly walk naked in the dark
after being clothed in ostrich feathers?

*

I am not a lunatic.
I wouldn't escape a wedding
only to sleep on ice,
for I know exactly which among my women
and my poems I desire,
and I know that nothing is new in the realm of
women.

فأنا أعرفُ دربي جيّداً... نحو أبراج الحَمَامِ...
وأنا أعرفُ من أرْضَعَني لبنَ العِشْقِ...
ومَنْ علّمني أحلى الكلامِ...
فاشْرَحي لي:
كيف أمضي هارباً من صدر أُمّي؟
ومن التُوتِ الذي يقطُرُ من حَلْمَتِها...
ومن الشمسِ التي تطلعُ من ضِحْكتِها...
كيف يا واحدتي؟
أرفضُ النَهْدَ الذي أطْعَمني
قصَبَ السُكرِ... والمانغُو... ونارَنْجَ الشآمِ؟
كيف أمشي عارياً تحت الظلامِ؟
وقميصي كانَ من ريشِ النَعَامِ؟؟...

*

لستُ مجذُوباً... لكيْ أهربَ من عُرْسٍ
وأبقى نائماً فوق الجليدْ...
فأنا أعرفُ بالتحديدِ ماذا
من حبيباتي أُريدْ...
ومن الشِعرِ أُريدْ...
وأنا أعرفُ...
أنْ لا شيءَ في العِلْمِ النِسَائيِّ... جديدْ!!.

Use your head, sweetheart.
I was never a Schariar, not even for a day.
I have never melted a woman's body with acid.
I was always a one–woman man,
a genuine lover with singular loyalty.
I am monotheistic in the religion of love;
I believe that love, in essence,
is the work of heavens.

*

I may have weird ambitions,
hobbies, and thoughts.
My greatest complex – from which I never
recovered –
is that every woman I adored
had to resemble my mother.

كَبِّري عقْلَكِ... يا سيِّدتي
فأنا ما كنتُ يوماً شَهْرَياراً...
لا ولا ذوّبتُ في الحامض أجسادَ النساءْ..
كنتُ دوماً رَجُلاً لامرأةٍ واحدةٍ...
وعشيقاً جيّداً... وأُحَادِيَّ الوَلَاءْ...
إنّني أؤمنُ بالتوْحيدِ في دينِ الهوى
وبأنَّ العشْقَ في جوهرِهِ...
هو شِعْرٌ من كتاباتِ السماءْ!!

*

ربَّما كانَتْ طُمُوحاتي غريبَهْ...
وهواياتي...
وأفكاري غريبَهْ...
عُقْدتي الكبرى التي لم أُشْفَ منها...
أنَّ كلَّ امرأةٍ أحبَبْتُها
كان لا بُدَّ بأن تُشْبِهَ أُميّ!!

My era has expired.
I have run out of Syrian roses,
Arabian mascara,
and French perfume.
I see before me
no hair cascading wildly on shoulders,
no breast that rises toward Allah.
Fatima no longer answers my call,
nor do Rawya and Ranya.
My authority does not extend to the musk vessels
and the songs of bracelets.
All the birds that I hid under my plaits have fled.

*

The era of Nizar has ended.
Love, as we knew it, has ended.
We entered into the era of Narcissism.
Lovers' memory has shrivelled,
and the <u>Mythical Lover</u> no longer remembers
the name of his sweetheart.

إنتهى العصرُ النزاريُّ ...
فلا وردٌ دمَشْقيٌ
ولا كُحْلٌ حِجَازيٌّ
ولا عطرٌ فَرَنسيٌّ
ولا شَعْرٌ على الأكتاف مجنُونٌ ...
ولا نهدٌ إلى اللّهِ ... يسَافرْ ...
خرجتْ فاطمةٌ عن طَاعَتي
خرجَتْ راويةٌ
خرجَتْ رانيةٌ
خرجَتْ عن سُلْطَتي ، أوعيةُ المِسْكِ .
وموسيقى الأساورْ ...
هَرَبتْ كلُّ العصافير التي خبَّأتُها
تحتَ الضفائرْ !!
*
إنتهى العصرُ النزاريُّ الذي عاصَرْتِهِ ...
وانتهى الحُبُّ كما نعرفُهُ ...
ودخلنا في زمان النرجسيَّةْ ...
يبستَتْ ذاكرةُ العشّاقِ ... حتى
لم يعدْ يذكرُ قَيْسٌ ...
إسْمَ ليلى العامريَّة !!

Lolita

1961

I have turned fifteen.
I have grown more beautiful –
a thousand times more.
and my love for you,
it too, has grown
a thousand times more.
For two years
you didn't pay attention
to my girlish ways –
my baby's face
and my skirts covering my knees.

*

I used to come to you
in my school uniform
and the crimson ribbon in my hair.
It used to be enough
that you gave me
a doll as a present,
or even candy.
I didn't ask for more.

لوليتا..

صارَ عُمّري خمسَ عَشْرهْ
صرتُ أحلى ألفَ مرّهْ
صار حُبّي لكَ أكبرْ
ألفَ مرّهْ ..
ربّما من سنَتَيْنْ
لم يكنْ تهتمُّ في وجهي المدّورْ
كان حُسْني بينَ بينْ ..
وفساتيني تُغطّي الرُكْبَتَيْنْ
*
كنتُ آتيكَ بثوبي المدرسْيّ
وشريطي القرمُزيّ
كان يكفيني بأن تُهْدي إليّ
دُمْيَةً .. قِطْعَةَ سُكَّرْ
لم أكنْ أطلُبُ أكثَرْ

Now that I've grown older,
I'm not satisfied
with candies or dolls.
The game has become more dangerous –
a thousand times more.
You have become my biggest toy,
my most challenging sport.
I have turned fifteen.

*

Everything within me has matured and blossomed,
everything has become vibrant green.
My lips have filled out,
and the breasts which were flat
two years ago
have today thrusted out in pride.
You just imagine the hot springs
and the pine forest in my body.

*

Yesterday's child
who used to play on your doorstep
and rest on your lap
when she was tired

وتطوَّرْ ..
بعد هذا كلُّ شيءٍ
لم أعُدْ أقنعُ في قطعة سُكَّرْ
ودُمَيً .. تطرحُها بين يديّ
صارت اللُّعْبَةُ أخطَرْ
ألفَ مرَّهْ ..
صرتَ أنتَ اللُّعْبَةَ الكُبرى لديّ
صرتَ أحلى لُعْبَةٍ بين يديّ
صار عُمري خمْسَ عَشْرَهْ

*

صار عُمْري خَمْسَ عَشْرَهْ
كُلُّ ما في داخلي .. غنَّى وأزهَرْ
كلُّ شيءٍ .. صارَ أخْضَرْ
شفتي خَوْخٌ .. وياقوتٌ مُكسَّرْ
وبصدري ضحكتْ قُبَّةُ مَرْمَرْ
وينابيعُ .. وشمسٌ .. وصنوبَرْ
صارتِ المرآة لو تلمسُ نهدي تتخدَّرْ
والذي كان سَوِيّاً قبل عامين تَدوَّرْ
فتصوَّرْ ...

*

طفلةُ الأمسِ التي كانتْ على بابكَ تلعبْ
والتي كانتْ على حضنكَ تغفو حين تتعبْ

has now become
a very expensive jewel
that cannot be priced.

*

I have turned fifteen;
I have become more beautiful.
You will ask me for a dance,
and I will be able to accept.
I will wear a striped shawl
and will look like an Arabian princess.
From now on
you won't feel uneasy.
I have grown taller –
how often I prayed
to grow taller,
just by the thickness of a finger or two,
and how often I tried
to look older,
just by a year or two.
Oh, how I hated my baby face
and the fringe on my school uniform.

*

Don't love me like a daughter.
Don't touch me like a daughter.
I have turned fifteen.

أصبحتْ قطعةَ جَوْهَرْ ..
لا تُقدَّرْ ...

*

صار عُمْري خَمْسَ عَشْرَهْ
صرتُ أجمَلْ ..
وستدعوني إلى الرقص .. وأقْبَلْ
سوفَ ألتفُّ بشالٍ قَصَبيّ
وسأبدو كالأميراتِ ببهو عربيّ ..
أنتَ بعد اليوم لن تخجلَ فيّ
فلقد أصبحتُ أطولْ ..
آهِ كم صلّيت كي أصبحَ أطولْ ..
إصبعاً .. أو إصبعينْ ..
سنةً أو سَنَتينْ ..
آه .. كم ثرتُ على وجهي المدوَّرْ
وذُؤاباتي .. وثوبي المدرسيّ
وعلى الحُبّ .. بشكلٍ أبَويّ

*

لا تعاملني بشكلٍ أبَويّ
فلقد أصبحَ عُمْري .. خَمْسَ عَشْرهْ

You Want

1996

You want, like all women,
the treasures of Solomon;
like all other women,
pools of perfume,
trunks of ivory combs
and a herd of slaves.
You want a master
who repeats your name
like a parrot,
who says *I Love You*
all day and all night,
and who, when you are weary,
washes your feet in wine.
Oh, Shehrazad of all women!

*

You desire, like all women,
the stars in the sky;
like all women,
platters of Menna
and Salwa
and stiletto shoes

تريدين ..

تُريدينَ مثلَ جميعِ النساءِ .
كنوزَ سليمانَ ..
مثلَ جميعِ النساءِ
وأحواضَ عطرٍ
وأمشاطَ عاجٍ
وسرْبَ إماءِ
تُريدينَ مَوْلىً ..
يُسبِّح باسمكِ كالبَبَغاءِ
يقولُ : (أحبُّكِ) عند الصباح
يقولُ : (أحبُّكِ) عند المساءِ
ويغسلُ بالخمر رجليْكِ ..
يا شهرزادَ النساءِ ..

*

تُريدينَ مثل جميعِ النساءِ
تُريدينَ مني نجومَ السماءِ
وأطباقَ مَنٍّ ..
وأطباقَ سلوى ..

made of chestnut flowers.
You want from Shanghai, its silk,
from Esfahan, its furs,
but I am not the prophet of prophets
who with his staff
divides the sea
and erects,
from a cluster of clouds,
a palace of glittering stones.

*

You want, like all women,
feather fans, kohl, and incense;
you want a very stupid slave
to recite poetry to you at bedtime.
You want –at the snap of your fingers –
the castle of al-Rashid,
the palace of Khosru
and a caravan of servants and retinues
to carry the train of your gowns.
Oh Cleopatra,
I am not who you think I am.
I am not Sinbad of the Skies.

وخُفَّيْنِ من زَهَرِ الكستناءِ ..
تريدينَ .. من شَنْغَهايَ الحريرَ ..
ومن أصفهانَ جلودَ الفراءِ ..
ولستُ نبيّاً من الأنبياءِ ..
لألقي عصايَ ..
فينشقُّ بحرٌ ..
ويولدُ بين الغمائمِ قصرٌ
جميعُ حجارتهِ من ضياءِ ..
*
تريدينَ مثلَ جميع النساءِ ..
مراوحَ ريشٍ
وكُحْلاً .. وعطرا ..
تريدينَ عبداً شديدَ الغباءِ
ليقرأ عند سريركِ شعرا..
تريدينَ في لحظتينِ اثْنَتَيْنِ
بلاطَ الرشيد وإيوانَ كِسرى
وقافلةً من عبيدٍ وأسرى
تجرُّ ذيولكِ .. يا كليْوبترا ..
ولستُ أنا ..
سندبادَ الفضاءِ ..

I cannot drop Babylon
and the pyramids
into your hands.
I don't possess Aladdin's lantern.
I can't offer you the sun on a platter
like all women wish.

*

Listen Shehrazad of all women,
I am nothing but a poor Damascene labourer;
I dip my bread in blood.
My understanding is simple
and so are my wages.
I believe in bread and the prophets,
and I dream of love like others –
of a wife who would stitch
the holes in my cloak –
of a child who would sleep in my lap
like a field bird or a water flower.

لأحضر بابلَ بين يديْكِ
وأهرامَ مصرِ .. وإيوانَ كِسْرى
وليس لديَّ سراجُ علاءِ
لآتيكِ بالشمسِ فوقَ إناءِ ..
كما تتمنَّى .. جميعُ النساءِ ..

*

وبعدُ ..
أيا شهرزادَ النساءِ ..
أنا عاملٌ من دمشقَ .. فقيرٌ
رغيفي أغمسُهُ بالدماءِ ..
شعوري بسيطٌ ، وأجري بسيطٌ
وأؤمنُ بالخبزِ والأولياءِ ..
وأحلُمُ بالحبِّ كالآخرينْ ..
وزوجٍ تخيطُ ثقوبَ ردائي ..
وطفلٍ ينامُ على ركبتيَّ
كعصفورِ حقلٍ ، كزهرةِ ماءِ ..

I think of love like others,
for love is like air,
and like the sun that shines
on the dreamers beyond the palace walls –
on the moiling and on the wretched,
whether they sleep fitfully in beds of silk
or wail in beds of rags.
You want, like all women,
the eighth wonder,
yet I own nothing
but my pride.

أفكِّر بالحبِّ كالآخرينْ ..
لأنَّ المحبَّة مثل الهواءِ ..
لأنَّ المحبَّة شمسٌ تضيء ..
على الحالمينَ وراء القصورِ ..
على الكادحينَ.. على الأشقياءِ .
ومَنْ يملكونَ سريرَ حريرِ
ومَنْ يملكونَ سريرَ بُكاءِ ..
تريدينَ مثلَ جميع النساءِ ..
تريدينَ ثامنةَ المعجزاتِ ..
وليس لديَّ ..
سوى كبريائي ..

To A Hireling

1956

With my money,
not with sweet nothings,
I ravished you.
Lured by the scent of my perfume
and exotic silks,
you hankered after me
like a blind starving cat.
You believed all my claims,
and before you knew what was happening,
your proud breasts
were among my trophies.

*

Where's your boastfulness
when I can control you
like the rings on my fingers?
I used to idolise your lips,
now they are there for my use.
I believed in beauty for hire;
I walked all over it with my good fortune.

إلى أ ِجيَرة

بدراهمي ..
لا بالحديث الناعمِ
حطّمتُ عزّتَكِ المنيعةَ كلّها بدراهمي
وبما حملتُ من النفائس والحرير الحالِمِ
فأطعتِــــني
وتبعتِــــني
كالقطّةِ العمياء ، مؤمنةً بكلّ مزاعمي
فإذا بصدرك ، ذلك المغرور ، ضمنَ غنائمي
*
أين اعتدادُكِ ؟
أنتِ أطوعُ في يدي من خاتمي
قد كان ثغرُكِ مرةً
ربّي ، فأصبح خادمي
آمنتُ بالحسن الأجير وطأتُهُ بدراهمي

I kicked it and humiliated it
with dolls and bangles,
with gold and velvets,
and glittering stones.
I dare you to resist.
Which part of your body
haven't I adorned with my treasures?
All the jewels on your breast
are only part of the price
I paid to watch you
stumble like a drunkard
into your inevitable fate.

*

I played with you.
Your lips never rebelled
against my vices,
and the two white bunnies
quivering atop your satin body
were too craven to cry out
while I was flaying them
with my torment and abuse.
I can't bear beauty
that cannot insult me back.

وركلتُهُ ، وذللتُهُ
بدُميً ، بأطواقٍ كوهم الواهِمِ
ذَهَبٌ وديباجٌ
وأحجارٌ تشعُّ .. فقاومي
أيُّ المواضع منكِ
لم تهطُلْ عليه غمائمي
خيراتُ صدرك كلُّها
من بعضِ بعضِ مواسمي ..
بدراهمي !
بإناء طيبٍ فاغمِ
ومشيتِ كالفأر الجبان إلى المصير الحاسمِ

*

ولهَوْتُ فيكِ فما انتختْ
شفتاكِ تحت جرائمي
والأرنبانِ الأبيضانِ
على الرخام الهاجِمِ
جبَنُا ..
فما شعرا بظلم الظالمِ ..
وأنا أصبُّ عليهما
ناري . ونارَ شتائمي
رُدّي .. فلست أطيقُ حُسناً
لا يردّ شتائمي !!

Pitiful thing.
I filled you full
and then drained you empty –
made of you an addict
under the influence
of a very expensive
and dangerous drug.

مسكينةٌ ..
لم يبقَ شيءٌ منكِ
منذُ استَعْبَدَتْكِ دراهمي ..

A Letter To An Anonymous Man

1961

Dear Sir,
This is a letter from a foolish woman.
Did you ever receive a letter from a foolish woman?
My name –
but what does it matter what my name is?
You can call me Rania, Zainab, Hind, or Haifa,
for aren't names our silliest possessions?

*

Sir,
I am afraid to say what I want.
I am afraid that if I did, the skies would burn.
Your East, my dear sir,
confiscates explicit letters.
It confiscates women's dreams and aspirations,
keeps women's emotions under house arrest,
uses the language of knives and hatchets to speak to women,
and slaughters spring, passion, and black pony tails.

رسـَالةِ إلى رَجُـــل مـــَا ..

يا سيّدي العزيزْ
هذا خطابُ امرأةٍ حمقاءْ ؟
هل كتبتْ إليكَ قبلي امرأةٌ حمقاءْ ؟
إسمي أنا ؟ دَعْنا من الأسماءْ
رانيةٌ .. أم زينبٌ
أم هندُ .. أم هيفاءْ
أسخفُ ما نحملُهُ – يا سيّدي – الأسماءْ

*

يا سيّدي
أخافُ أن أقولَ ما لديَّ من أشياءْ
أخافُ – لو فعلتُ –
أن تحترقَ السماءْ ..
فشرقُكمْ يا سيّدي العزيزْ
يصادرُ الرسائلَ الزرقاءْ
يصادرُ الأحلامَ من خزائن النساءْ
يمارسُ الحَجْرَ على عواطف النساءْ
يستعملُ السكّينَ ..
والساطورَ ..
كي يخاطبَ النساءْ
ويذبحُ الربيعَ ، والأشواقَ ..
والضفائرَ السوداءْ
وشرقكمْ يا سيّدي العزيزْ

Your East, dear sir,
brandishes women's skulls as their trophies of
honour.

*

Do not condemn me, Dear Sir, if my handwriting
is poor,
for I am writing while the executioner is at my
doorstep,
amidst the sound of howling winds and barking
dogs.
Dear Sir, the <u>Black Knight</u> is at my doorstep.
He would imprison me if he laid eyes on this
letter.
He would slay me if he caught a glimpse of my
underwear,
and he would decapitate me if I aired my
grievances.
Your East, my dear sir, lays siege to women, with
honed spears.
Your East, dear sir, appoints men as prophets and
buries women in dirt.

*

يصنعُ تاجَ الشرفِ الرفيع
مِنْ جماجمِ النساءْ ..
*
لا تنتقدْني سيّدي
إن كانَ خطّي سيئاً ..
فإنَّني أكتبُ والسيّافُ خلفَ بابي
وخارجَ الحجرة صوتُ الريحِ والكلابِ..
يا سيّدي !
عنترةُ العبسيُّ خلفَ بابي
يذبحُني ..
إذا رأى خطابي ..
يقطعُ رأسي ..
لو رأى الشفّافَ من ثيابي ..
يقطعُ رأسي ..
لو أنا عبَّرتُ عن عذابي ..
فشرقُكمْ يا سيّدي العزيزْ
يحاصرُ المرأةَ بالحرابِ ..
وشرقكمْ ، يا سيّدي العزيزْ
يبايعُ الرجالَ أنبياءً
ويطمرُ النساءَ في الترابِ ..
*

Don't be upset, my dear sir, by what I have to say.
Don't be upset if I have broken from my age–old confines
and removed your seal from my conscience, or
if I have fled from the harem's quarter
and rebelled against my inevitable death –
my sealed tomb, my heritage and the vast slaughterhouse.
Don't be upset, Sir,
if I have exposed my innermost feelings,
for I know the Eastern man is not attuned to feelings and emotions.
The Eastern man – excuse me if I'm blunt –
recognises women only in bed.

*

Excuse me, Sir, if I dare to challenge the kingdom of men,
for everyone knows that real literature can only be written by men!
Love has always belonged to men,

لا تنزعجْ !
يا سيّدي العزيزَ .. من سُطوري
لا تنزعجْ !
إذا كسرتُ القمقمَ المسدودَ من عصور .
إذا نزعتُ خاتمَ الرَصَاص عن ضميري
إذا أنا هربتُ
من أقبية الحريمِ في القصور ..
إذا تمرَّدتُ ، على موتي ..
على قبري ، على جذوري ..
والمسلخِ الكبير ...
لا تنزعجْ ، يا سيّدي
إذا أنا كشفتُ عن شعوري ..
فالرجلُ الشرقيُّ
لا يهتمُّ بالشِعْرِ ولا الشعور ..
الرجلُ الشرقيُّ
-واغفِرْ جرأتي-
لا يفهمُ المرأةَ إلا داخلَ السرير ..

*

معذرةً يا سيّدي
إذا تطاولتُ على مملكة الرجالِ
فالأدبُ الكبيرُ - طبعاً- أدبُ الرجالِ
والحبُّ كان دائماً
من حصَّةِ الرجالِ ..

and sex has always been a sedative sold
freely to men.
Women's freedom is a myth in our countries;
the only freedom we own exists in our heads.
Sir, you can call me names if you wish,
for I don't care.
You can call me crazy, stupid, vapid –
any name at all – because I don't care anymore.
Because in the logic of men,
only a foolish woman would so openly recount
her dilemma.
Anyway, didn't I mention in the beginning
that this was a letter from a foolish woman?

والجِنْسُ كان دائماً
مُخدِّراً يُباعُ للرجالِ ..
خرافةٌ حرِّيةُ النساءِ في بلادنا
فليس من حريةٍ
أخرى ، سوى حريَّة الرجالِ ..
يا سيّدي ..
قُلْ كلَّ ما تريده عنّي . فلنْ أُبالي
سطحيَّةٌ . غبيَّةٌ . مجنونةٌ . بلهاءْ
فلم أعُدْ أُبالي ..
لأنَّ من تكتبُ عن همومها ..
في منطق الرجال تدعى امرأةً حمقاءْ
ألمْ أقلْ في أوّل الخطاب إني امرأةٌ حمقاءْ

Pregnant

1956

Don't be mad, I said.
I'll be brief –
I think I'm pregnant.
And you yelled like a madman,
We'll destroy it,
and you went on
cursing me
and wanted to throw me out.
I'm not surprised,
I always knew
what a bastard you were,
and then you ordered your servant
to push me into the dreary road.

حُبْــلَى

لا تمتقعْ !
هيَ كلْمةٌ عجْلى
إني لأشعرُ أنني
حُبْلى ! !
وصرختَ كالملسوع بي :
"كلاّ" !
سنمزّق الطفلا
وأردتَ تطرُدُني
وأخذتَ تشتمني
لا شيء يدهشُني
فلقد عَرَفتُكَ دائماً نذْلا ..
وبعثتَ بالخدّام يدفعني
في وحشة الدربِ

Oh, you're the one
who sowed the seeds
of shame in me
and broke my heart.
You sent him to tell me
that you were not there.
You were indeed there,
but you cowered
when you realised
that I am pregnant.

*

What? Are you going to spit me out?
The vomit in my mouth
is destroying me
and the nausea is suffocating me
while your condemned heir
is inside me,
disgrace is besieging me;
a dark fact is filling me.

*

يا مَنْ زرعتَ العارَ في صُلبْي .
وكسرتَ لي قلبي
ليقولَ لي :
"مولايَ ليسَ هُنا .."
مولاهُ ألفُ هنا ..
لكنَّه جَبُنَا
لما تأكَّد أنني حُبلى
*
مـــــاذا ؟
أتبصُقني ؟
والقيءُ في حلقي يدمِّرني
وأصابعُ الغَثَيان تخنقني
ووريثكَ المشؤوم في بدني
والعارُ يسحقني
وحقيقةٌ سوداءُ تملؤني
هي أنني .. حُبْلى
*

I laugh at your money.
What's it for,
for aborting me
or mummifying me?
Is that what I'm worth?
Is that what my loyalty is worth?
You reeking rogue,
I did not come to get
your stinking money.
(No thanks)
I will abort what you made me conceive;
I don't want him a damned father.

ليراتُكَ الخمسون .. تضحكني .
لمَن النقودُ .. لمنْ :
لتُجهضَني ؟
لتخيطَ لي كفَني ؟
هذا إذن ثمني ؟
ثمنُ الوفا يا بؤرة العَفَن
أن لم أجِئْكَ لمالِك النَتِن
"شكراً" ..
سأُسقطُ ذلك الحَمْلا ..
أنا لا أريدُ له أباً نذْلا ..

Vessels Of Pus

1956

Him: No–No, I don't want to.
For the fiftieth time, I told you, I don't want –
Her: And you dived into your pillow,
you turned your face to the wall.
You left me behind you seething,
blood bursting my veins.
My hair is cascading over my shoulders.
The wind is rattling the door handle.
The dogs are barking faraway,
and your nightly guard is snoozing
while water is pouring from the roof spouts –
a perfectly orchestrated setting.

*

You have even stolen the blanket.
You have plundered my orchard,
the fruit of which you so greedily devoured
when it was freshly ripe and pungent with seed.

أوْعيَة الصّدِيد

"لا .. لا أُريدْ"
"المرَّةُ الخمسون .. إنيَ لا أُريدْ"
ودفنتَ رأسكَ في المخدَّة يا بليدْ ..
وأدرتَ وجهكَ للجدارِ ..
أيا جداراً من جليدْ
وأنا وراءَكَ ..
يا صغيرَ النفس .. نابحةُ الوريدْ
شعري على كتفي بديدْ
والريحُ تفتل مقبضَ الباب الوصيدْ
ونباحُ كلبٍ من بعيدْ
والحارسُ الليليُّ .. والمزرابُ متّصل النشيدْ

*

حتى الغطاءَ سرقتَهُ ..
وطعنتَ لي الأملَ الوحيدْ

You have gorged yourself on my only possession,
and now you want to spit me out.
Just a moment ago,
you were raging across the room
like a bull,
but now you are beside me –
a mass of dead meat.
Oh, how despicable dead meat is!

*

What do I want?
You, the Heir of The Sultan Abdul_Hameed,
laying around the Turkish muttaka
with your Circassian harem,
watching one beautiful head after another
fall onto your carpet,
while even the lazy narghile
is unable to put up with you.
You, The Caliph
of the Islamic Nation,
the merry king,
you who spoil then discard
whomever you like – no matter whom.

أملي الذي مزّقتَه .. أملي الوحيدْ
مـــــاذا أُريدْ ؟
و قُبَيْلَ ثانيتين كنت تجولُ كالثور الطريدْ
والآن أنتَ بجانبي
قفصٌ من اللحمِ القديدْ ..
ما أشنعَ اللحمَ القديدْ
*
ماذا أريدْ ؟
يا وارثاً عبدَ الحميدْ
والمتّكى التركيُّ
والنرجيلةُ الكسلى تئنُّ وتستعيدْ
والشركسيّاتُ السبايا حول مضجعه الرغيدْ
يسقُطْنَ فوق بساطه .. جيداً فجيدْ
وخليفةُ الإسلام والملكُ السعيدْ
يرمي .. ويأخذ ما يريدْ

Oh no.
Abdul_Hameed did not die.
Abdul_Hameed lives in you.
Especially in here,
in this wrought and gilded bed,
we women become your slaves.
How many breasts have withered
beneath your lashes?
How many shaped bellies
wept from your provocation?

*

What do you think I want?
Nothing –
Murderer. Pirate. Frigid man.
I am but a vessel for your pus
oh, alas the vessels of pus!

لا .. لم يمتْ عبدُ الحميدْ
فلقد تقمَّصَ فيكُمُ عبدُ الحميدْ
حتى هنا ..
حتى على السُرُرِ المقوَّسة الحديدْ
نحنُ النساءَ لكمْ عبيدْ
وأحطُّ أنواع العبيدْ ..
كم ماتَ تحت سياطكمْ نهدٌ شهيدْ
وبكى من استئثاركمْ
خصرٌ عميدْ
*
مـــــاذا أُريدْ ؟
لا شيءَ ..
يا سفَّاحُ . يا قرصانُ . يا قَبْوَ الجليدْ
فأنا وعاءٌ للصديدْ
يا ويلَ أوعيةِ الصديدْ
هيَ ليس تملكُ أن تريدَ ولا تريدْ ..

The Arsonist Of Rome

1970

Please stop talking.
Your drivel is driving me mad.
What shall I call what you did –
sadism,
opportunism,
piracy,
or just plain meanness?
What shall I call it, woman,
this mixing of love with trade,
integrity with whoredom –
what shall I call it?
No matter how I try, words escape me.
You have set the whole of Rome afire
just to light a cigarette.

حارقـــة رومـــا

كُفّي عن الكلام يا ثرثارَهْ ..
كُفّي عن المشْي ..
على أعصابيَ المنهارَهْ
ماذا أُسمّي كلَّ ما فعلتِهِ ؟
ساديَّةٌ ..
نفعيَّةٌ ..
قرصنةٌ ..
حقارَهْ ..
ماذا أُسمّي كلَّ ما فعلتِهِ ؟
يا مَنْ مزجتِ الحبَّ بالتجارَهْ
والطهرَ بالدعارَهْ ..
ماذا أُسمّي كلَّ ما فعلتِهِ ؟
فإنّني لا أجِدُ العبارَهْ
أحرقتِ روما كلهَّا
لتُشعلي سجارَهْ ..

Clown

1966

Now that you've found another lover,
you say you want to be friends.
And you say it so clumsily,
your face brazen, your eyes
fixed everywhere but on me.
You know me well enough to understand
I won't put up with this,
so get out of my way.
You lost soul –
what you suggest is really funny.
You should be a comedian,
although you deserve pity
more than applause.

*

For five years I've nourished you
on the nectar of my love,
have become, for your sake,
the very air that you breathe,
and now you say *Let's be friends*.

مُهَرّجـــة

أتريدينَ إذْ وجدتِ العشيقا
أتريدينَ أن أكونَ صديقا ؟
وتقولينَها بكلّ غباءٍ
بؤبؤاً جامداً .. ووجهاً صفيقا
موقفي تعرفينهُ . فَتَوارَيْ
عن طريقي ، يا مَنْ أضعتِ الطريقا
مُضْحِكٌ ما اقترحتِ . يا بهلواناً
يستحقُّ الــرثاءَ .. لا التصفيقا
*
أصديقٌ .. وبعدَ خمس سنينٍ
كنتُ فيهـــا الشذا وكنتُ الرحيقا
يالهُ منطقُ النســاء . أمثــلي
يقبلُ الآن أن يكونَ صديقا ؟

How sick is your logic, woman!
And how stupid.
Just ask your breasts
about my fingerprints
I have set fire to each one,
and just like that
we are brother and sister.
As if I hadn't filled your cleavage
with every inch of my manhood.
As if I hadn't spilled my salt
in every crevice of your body.

*

Rest assured that I won't
pretend how I feel about this.
It is the fate of the eagle
to soar freely.
I will never be a domesticated kitten
to whom you bend to stroke whenever
the urge strikes you,
or an old dress you finger sentimentally
when you air your closets.
I was always the master in my love ceremonies.
It won't be easy to make a fool of me.

إسألي ناهدَيْكِ عن بَصَماتي
كلُّ نهدٍ ، أشعلتُ فيه حريقا
هكذا . بين ليلةٍ وضُحاها ..
نتلاقى شقيقةً .. وشقيقا
فكأني لم أملأ الصدرَ لوزاً ..
وعلى الثغر ما سكبتُ العقيقا
*
إطمئنّي .. فلن أزوِّرَ نفسي
قَدَرُ النسر أن يظلّ طليقا
أبداً .. لن أكون قطاً أليفاً
تستضيفينَهُ .. وثـــوباً عتيقا
سيّداً كنتُ في مقاصير حُبّي
ومن الصعب أن أصير رقيقا

A Voice From The Harem

1961

You love me!
Those same hollow words.
You love me!
That same hackneyed cliché.
You love me!
That same old tune you
intoxicated me with the
first time we met.
Your words no longer move me.
I am numb
and have forgotten
what love means.

*

You love me!
Yes. I believe you!
Just like you love
any other woman you see.

صَوْتٌ مِنَ الحَريم

"تُحبُّني" !
الجُمْلَةُ الجوفاءُ ذاتُها .. "تُحِبُّني"
اللفْظَةُ البلهاءُ ذاتُها .. "تُحِبُّني"
النغمةُ القديمةُ التي بها دوَّخْتَنَي
أوَّلَ ما عَرَفْتَني
أضعتُ إحساسي بها ..
فلم تعُدْ تهزُّني ..
*
"تُحِبُّني" .
كأيِّ .. أيِّ امرأةٍ تُحِبُّني

I'm simply another face
in your colouring book,
a newspaper you'll read
with relish, then leave
to fade on your table,
an iris you planted
in your field of varieties,
a porcelain doll you'll
play with until
another comes along.

*

You love me!
Please stop making
a fool of yourself.
You are like
a circus player
with thousands of masks
and a million consummate roles.
Enough. Enough.
I've lived this play
long enough.

وجهٌ أنا .. وجهٌ من الوُجُوه في دفتركَ المُلوَّنِ
جريدةٌ صفراءُ تطويني إذا قرأتَني
سَوْسَنَةٌ تُضيفُها إلى ألوفِ السَوْسَنِ ..
ولُعْبةٌ من وَرَقٍ .. تشيلُني ..
تَحُطُّني
فإنْ رأيتَ لعبةً جديدةً
حَطَّمَتني ..

*

"تُحبُّني" !
لا .. لا تُعِدْها مرةً أخرى .. فقد أضْحَكْتَني
يا لاعباً في السِرْكِ .. يا مُهَرِّجاً
بألف وجهٍ مُسْتَعَارٍ .. ألفِ دورٍ متْقَنِ ..
كَفى .. كَفَى .. فتلك مسرحيَّةٌ
مثَّلتَها أوَّلَ ما رأيتَني .

For two years now
I've watched you perform
and have been enchanted
with each one of your acts.
The set and special effects
were superb.
And the script!
How rich were the theatrics,
how bright the stage!
You kept me on the edge
of my seat until I heard
your first hollow line,
the false rhythms
of an alphabet
only you could have created.
And what, I ask you,
is more useless
than a false alphabet?

*

You love me!
If you only knew
how common that melody is,
how fraudulent its composer.

وعشتُ عامَيْنِ بها ..
مأخوذةً بكُلِّ ما أسْمَعْتَني
بالضوءِ ، بالحوارِ ، بالجوِّ الروائيِّ الغني
فَمَشْهَدٌ يقيمُني
ومَشْهَدٌ يُقْعِدُني
وأنتَ ، فوقَ المسرح المُضاءِ تَستَثيرُني
بالجُمَلِ الجوفاءِ .. بالحرف الذي لم يُؤمِنِ ..
ما أرخَصَ الحرفَ إذا لم يُؤمِنِ

*

"تُحبُّني" !
معزوفةٌ معادةٌ رخيصةُ المُلحِّنِ

Yet you keep playing it
to every pretty face
in the audience.
Say something else
before you shatter
what's left of my nerves.
Say anything else.
Say you like the scent
of my perfume,
the warmth and colour
of my home.
Say that I'm beautiful,
easy to talk to,
and that I gave you
everything you asked for.
Blindly, yes,
and unfortunately,
everything you asked for.
Why can't you admit it?
Why can't you say what
my true worth is –
that of a conquest
you'll eventually bury
beyond the walls of
an eternal harem.

تُديرُها .. تُديرها لكلِّ وجهٍ حَسَنِ
قُلْ غيرَها ..
أتْلَفْتَ أعصابي بها ..
أتْلَفْتَني ...
قُلْ غَيْرَها ..
قُلْ تشتهي طيبي .. ودفءَ مَسْكَني
قُلْ إنَّني ..
جميلةٌ .. وسَهْلَةٌ .. وإنَّني
أعطيتُ في بلاهةٍ جميعَ ما سألتَني
واأسفي .. جميعَ ما سألتَني ..
تريدُني ..
محظيَّةً جديدةً
تدفُنُها .. وراء جدران الحريمِ المُزْمِنِ ..

I'm sorry, my dear exploiter,
but I need more than that.
I need a man who will love me
more than he loves
the sound of his own words,
a man who is more than
an avid collector,
specialising in eyes.
A man who will prize me more
than the strand of coloured beads
he holds so joyfully
in the folds of his lap.

أما أنا فإنّني ..
أبحثُ يا مُسْتَتَثْمري ..
عَنْ رجُلٍ يُحبُّني ..
وأنتَ لا تعرفُ أن تُحِبَّ .. أنْ تُحِبَّني .
فأنتَ غاوي تُحَفٍ ..
ميدانُكَ العيونُ .. لا ما وراءَ الأعيُنِ
وأنتَ طفْلٌ لاعبٌ
بالخَرَزِ الملوَّنِ ..

A Bedside Sermon Behind The Closed Doors

1989

Forgive me if I let you down in love,
for I am not like other lovers.
The sword of sorrows has riddled my soul,
and yet, you are love–hungry.
I have deciphered the nature of things
and fathomed the gulfs and the depths.
I have explored forests in the orient and west
and harvested grapes and peaches.
So take respite from your struggle.
What love is inexhaustible?
Temper the fervour of your breasts.
I am neither in a hurry nor overwhelmed by
desire.
Never was I unmanly. Never.
Nor was I dunce or debilitated.
Still, I haven't vowed celibacy or embraced
escapism,
for I remain a contender in the race.
But I cannot allow myself to fake love
or practise hypocrisy.
I don't pursue bland intercourse,
for one has to observe the ethics of sex.

محاضرة في غرفة نوم مُغْلَقَة

سَامِحيني .. إذا خذلتُكِ في الحُبِّ .
فإنّي لا أُشْبِهُ العُشّاقا ..
إنَّ سيفَ الأحزانِ ، يفتحُ في الرُوحِ
ثُقُوباً .. وما شَبِعْتِ عِنَاقا
قد حفظتُ الأشياءَ عن ظهر قلبٍ
ودرستُ الخُلْجَانَ .. والأعماقا
واكْتَشَفْتُ الغَابَات .. شرقاً وغَرْباً
وقطفتُ الأعْنَابَ .. والدُرّاقا
فاستريحي .. من الكفاحِ قليلاً
أيُّ حُبٍّ لا يعرفُ الإرْهَاقا ؟
خَفّفي من حماسِ نَهْدَيْكِ .. إنّي
لستُ مُسْتَعْجلاً .. ولا مُشْتَاقا
لم أكُنْ فاقدَ الرجولة يوماً
لا ولا كنتُ أبْلَهاً .. أو مُعَاقَا ..
ليسَ هذا تصوُّفاً .. أو هُرُوباً
فأنا – بَعْدُ – ما خسرتُ السِبَاقا
غيرَ أنّي في الحُبِّ ، لا أقْبَلُ الغِشَّ
ونَفْسي ، لا تستطيبُ النفاقَا
لستُ أبْغي جَنْساً بغير مِزَاجٍ
إنَّ للجِنْسِ ، دائماً ، أخْلاَقَا ...

The Runners

1995

The last wall of shame collapsed.
We rejoiced.
We danced.
And we shook each other's hands
as we signed the treaty of the cowards.
Nothing will terrify us anymore,
and nothing will humiliate us anymore,
for our veins of pride have bled dry.

*

For the fiftieth time
our virginity was violated.
We didn't tremble. We didn't cry,
and we didn't cringe at the sight of blood.
We entered into the era of running.
We stood in lines
like sheep before the slaughterhouse.
We ran; we gasped for air,
and we rushed to kiss the shoes of the executioner.

*

المُهرولُون

سقطَتْ آخرُ جُدران الحياءْ ..
وفرحنا ..
ورقصنا ..
وتباركنا بتوقيع سلام الجُبناءْ ..
لا يعد يرعبنا شيءٌ ..
فقد يبست فينا عروقُ الكبرياءْ ..
*
سقطتْ ..
- للمرة الخمسين - عُذريتنا ..
دون أن نهتزّ .. أو نصرخ ..
أو يرعبنا مرأى الدماء
ودخلنا في زمان الهروَلة ..
ووقفنا بالطوابير ، كأغنامٍ أمام المقصلة .
وركضْنا .. ولَهثْنا ..
وتسابقنا لتقبيل حذاءِ القَتَلة ..
*

They starved our children for fifty years
and at the end of our fast,
they threw us an onion.

*

Granada fell
For the fiftieth time
out of the hands of the Arabs –
even the history books fell
out of the hands of the Arabs.
And so did the pillars of hope:
The limbs of our tribe,
and the preludes of our songs of glory.
Seville,
Antakya,
Hittin – without the glorious battle –
and Ammoria;
they all fell.
The Virgin Mary fell into the hands of the militias
and there was no man to rescue her –
there was not one man capable.

*

جوّعوا أطفالنا خمسين عاماً
ورموا في آخر الصوم إلينا ..
بَصَلة ..

*

سَقطتْ غرناطةٌ
– للمرة الخمسين – من أيدي العرب
سقط التاريخ من أيدي العرب
سقطت أعمدة الروح..وأفخاذ القبيلة..
سقطتْ كلُّ مواويل البطولة..
سقطت أشبيليه..
سقطت أنطاكيهُ..
سقطت حطين من غير قتالٍ..
سقطت عمورية ..
سقطت مريم في أيدي الميليشيات،
فما من رجل ينقذ الرمز السماوي،
ولا ثم رُجولة ..

*

The last of the concubines has fallen
into the hands of the Romans.
So whom shall we protect now?
There remains not a single concubine in the palace!
Who will make us coffee
and open her legs to us at night?
So whom shall we protect now?

*

There remains in our hands
no single Andalusia.
They've stolen the doors and the walls,
the wives and the children,
the olives and the oil,
and the stones in the streets.
They've kidnapped Jesus
while he was breast–feeding.
They've stolen even our memories
of the lemon tree,
apricots and mint,
and the lanterns of the mosques.

سقطت آخر محظياتنا
في يد الروم، فعن ماذا نُدافع ؟
لم يعُد في قصرنا جارية واحدة .
تصنع القهوة .. والجنس ..
فعن ماذا ندافع ؟؟
*
لم يعُدْ في يدنا ..
أندلس واحدة نملكُها
سرقُوا الأبواب،
الحيطان،
والزوجات، والأولاد،
والزيتون، والزّيتَ
وأحجار الشوارعْ ..
سرقوا عيسى بن مريمْ
وهو مازال رضيعاً
سرقوا ذاكرةَ الليمون ..
والمشمش..والنعناع منّا ..
وقناديل الجوامع ..

They handed us a tin of sardine, called Gaza,
a dry bone called Jericho,
a hotel – without pillars or a roof –
called Palestine.
They left us with a body without bones
and a hand without fingers.
There remain no ruins to cry over,
but can we cry
when even our tear ducts have been stolen?

*

After this secret love affair in Oslo,
we returned home impotent and barren.
They tailored and gift wrapped for us a nation
smaller than a grain of wheat,
a nation we could swallow without water,
like aspirin.

*

After fifty years of diaspora,
we squat on derelict land,
homeless and wandering
like a pack of dogs.

*

تركوا عُلبة سردين بأيدينا
تسمى (غزة)..
عظمة يابسة تُدعى (أريحا) ..
فندقاً يُدعى فلسطين،
بلا سقف ولا أعمدة ..
تركونا جَسداً دون عظامٍ
ويدا دون أصابع ..
*
لم يعدْ ثمَّةَ أطلالٌ لكي نبكي عليها
كيف.. تبكي أمة ..
أخذوا منها المدامع؟
*
بعدَ هذا الغَزَل السريّ، في أوسلُو
خرجنا عاقرين..
وهبُونا وطناً أصغر من حبة قمحٍ..
وطناً نبلعُهُ من غير ماءٍ
كحبُوب الأسبرينْ !!
*
بعد خمسين سنةً..
نجلس الآن، على الأرض الخرابْ
ما لنا مأوى.. كآلاف الكلابْ..
*

After fifty years of diaspora,
we still have no home to call our own,
unless its name is "The Mirage".
You can't call this dagger ripping out our guts
peace,
it is an act of rape.

*

Why the haste?
What good will this running do us
when the conscience of the masses remains
ticking
like the timer of the bomb,
and when the heft of signatures at Oslo
adds up to the weight of a mustard seed?

*

How often we dreamt of a green peace,
a white crescent,
a blue sea,
and the promised castles.
But without warning, we found ourselves
face down in a dung heap.

*

بعد خمسين سنة ..
ما وجدنا وطناً نسكنُه
إلا السراب ..
ليس صُلحاً ..
ذلك الصلح الذي أدخل كالخنجر فينا .
إنه فعْل اغتصاب!!
*
ما تفيدُ الهرْولة؟
ما تُفيد الهرولة؟
عندما يبقى ضمير الشعب حياً
كفتيل القُنبلة ..
لن تساوى كل توقيعات أوسلُو ..
خَردَلَة!!
*
كم حَلُمنا بسلامٍ أخضرٍ ..
وهلال أبيض
وبحر أزرق.
وقُلُوع مرسلة ..
ووجدنا فجأة أنفُسنا
في مزبلة!!
*

I wonder who will question them
about the peace of the cowards.
I wonder who will question them
about this peace that was sold by installments,
leases, and business deals.
Who will ask the CEOs and the investors
about this peace of the dead?
They cleared the streets,
silenced the murmuring,
and murdered the questions.

*

We married without love
the female who one day ate our children.
She feasted on our livers,
and then we carried her off on a honeymoon.
We drank, danced,
and recited our favourite love poems.
We sired, to our sorrow,
children who looked like frogs.

من تُرى يسألهم
عن سلام الجُبناء؟؟
لا سلام الأقوياء القادرين ..
من تُرى يسألهم؟
عن سلام البيع بالتقسيط،
والتأجير بالتقسيط ..
والصفقات ..
والتجار.. والمستثمرين؟
من تُرى يسألهم؟
عن سلام الميتين ..
أسكتوا الشارع ..
واغتالوا جميع الأسئلة ..
وجميع السائلين ..

*

وتزوّجنَا بلا حُبّ..
من الأنثى التي ذات يومٍ، أكلت أولادنا .
مضغت أكبادنا ..
وأخذناها إلى شهر العسلْ ..
وسكرنا .. ورقصنا ..
واستعدنا كل ما نحفظ من شعر الغزلْ .
ثم أنجبنا-لسؤ الحظ-أولاداً معاقين ..
لهم شكل الضفادع ..

We were lost in the diaspora of grief
with no land to call home
and no child to embrace.
At this wedding,
there was no Arabian dancing,
no Arabian food,
no Arabian songs,
and no Arabian dignity.
And none of our neighbourhood boys
joined the wedding procession.

*

Half of the dowry was paid for in dollars,
and so was the diamond ring.
The wedding cake was a present from America;
the bridal veil, the flowers, the candles,
and the wedding march of the Marine Corp Band
were all made in the USA.

*

وتشرّدنا على أرصفة الحزن ..
فلا من بَلد نحضُنُهُ..
أو من وَلَد!!
لم يكُن في العرسِ رقصٌ عربيٌّ
أو طعام عربيٌّ
أو غناءٌ عربي
أو حياءٌ عربي
فلقد غابَ عن الزّفَّةِ أولادُ البلد ..
*
كان نصفُ المهر بالدولار ..
كان الخاتم الماسي بالدولار ..
كانت أجرة المأذون بالدولار ..
والكعكة كانت هبة من أمريكا
وغطاء العُرس، والأزهارُ، والشمعُ،
وموسيقى المارينز ..
كلها قد صنعت في أمريكا ..
*

The wedding was over,
but Palestine did not attend the reception.
And yet she watched the taped footage
televised on all the world's channels.
And she watched as her tears traversed the oceans
towards Chicago, New Jersey, and Miami,
like a fallen bird bewailing its impending death.
This wedding gown doesn't fit me.
This shame is not mine.
Oh never, America. Oh never, America. Oh never, America.

وانتهى العرسُ.. ولم
تحضر فلسطين الفَرَحّ
بل رأت صورتها مبثوثة عبرَ كل الأقنية .
ورأت دمعتها تعبرُ أمواجَ المحيط ..
نحو شيكاغو.. وجيرسي .. وميامي ..
وهي مثل الطابور المذبوح تصرخ:
ليس هذا العُرس عُرسي..
ليس هذا الثوب ثوبي
ليس هذا العار عاري..
أبداً.. يا أمريكا..
أبداً.. يا أمريكا..
أبداً يا أمريكا..

My Encounter with Nizar Kabbani

My love of Nizar Kabbani's beautiful and enthralling poetry has been an integral part of my life for many years, and I established an interest in translating his poetry into English before I met this giant of poetry. My American editor, the fine poetess Lisa Kavchak, was equally immersed in studying Arabic literature and loved Kabbani's poetry, especially his political writings. Until I read the article in the London–based Arabic daily *Al–Hayat* (18 August 1995), I was unaware of Mr Kabbani's reluctance to have his poems translated. In that article, Kabbani cited 21 reasons not to translate poetry (see translation of the article on p. 221).

I recall with joy my first encounter with Kabbani. It was the 12 of December 1995, in the Gulf State of Bahrain. Mr Kabbani was a guest of the Ministry of Cabinet Affairs and Information, who welcomed him to honour them with a reading of his poetry. I had by then translated – purely as a hobby and an engrossing one at that – a variety of around 20 of his poems with Lisa kindly fine–tuning my efforts.

Kabbani's fans are numerous and this was nowhere more evident than at the spectacular poetry reading in which almost five thousand ardent poetry lovers attended. Even the then newly opened Holiday Inn Conference Centre could not accommodate everyone, cavernous though it is.

Hundreds of people had to stand for two hours, and many more were stranded outside the hall because of the over–crowding. Cars blocked the roads of Manama's Diplomatic Area, which led to the Conference Centre, and car parks were full at that off–peak hour of the evening. The audience was rapt as Kabbani recited many of his new political works and a lesser number of his love poems. However, this situation is incomparable to his open–air poetry reading in Sudan. Ten thousand people attended that event, and according to Kabbani, "They were dangling like clusters of black grapes."

I had struggled to meet the poet through the ordinary channels to no avail. To my knowledge, there was not a single press interview with Kabbani. And to make matters worse, there was an impenetrable ring of bureaucracy and red tape surrounding the poet's room at Le Royal Meridien in Manama as was befitting this superstar of the literary world.

So in a fit of bravura, I decided to contact him directly from the hotel's lobby using my mobile telephone. I asked him if Lisa and I could meet for few minutes to show him a draft translation of this collection of his poems. He answered me with his husky voice (I could hardly believe I was talking to the great man himself), and knowing that we were already in the hotel lobby, he asked us to come to his room. I had earlier written him a short note explaining the project in brief and requesting his permission for publication. As we entered, his room was inundated with flowers and baklavas from his enthusiasts.

After welcoming us, he quickly browsed through the draft book and promised that he would write to us. After a short while, he said, "Let me be open with you, I don't mind you translating my love poems, but I insist that no translation is made of my political poetry." Lisa, who much admires his political writings, inquired why this was. "Why should we show the world our dirty laundry?" replied the poet adamantly.

We were more than satisfied and so exhilarated at the outcome of this encounter, that I had no choice but to accept his offer and do without the political poems. Hence, we had to omit several political poems, and after doing our homework and reviewing most of his collections, we added 20 more of his greatest love poems to recompense for the lost political works.

In April 1996, I was in London for a short break. My friend Adnan Yousif, the former Information Attaché at the Bahrain Embassy in London had notified the poet of my arrival. Mr Kabbani asked Mr Yousif if we could call on him. "Bring your friend Nayef along for coffee, I have a few things to tell him", said the famous poet. So my second encounter gracefully permitted by the poet lasted a full hour, and was more productive than I could have hoped for. The poet expressed appreciation over the draft copy, which he perused thoroughly and approved in principle the work done on specific poems. He also praised, in absence, Lisa for her adaptations, re–creations and fine–tuning.

Kabbani re–iterated his condition of not translating the political poems, asking us to concentrate on love poems, which he felt would be acceptable to readers of different backgrounds. He also wanted his biography to be based on a brochure published in Bahrain by the Ministry of Cabinet Affairs and Information on the occasion of his visit.

He strongly recommended translating his latest love poems that appeared in *Al–Hayat,* and proposed translating as many as 30 poems so that he could eventually select around 20 for the book. Kabbani stressed that the book be completely bilingual and preferred that the Arabic text and English translation be printed on pages facing each other. He suggested that he handwrite the Arabic verse himself but unfortunately, his untimely demise before the completion of the project has precluded the fulfillment of this wish.

As an example of what he wished the book to look like, he presented me with a book entitled *Nizar Kabbani–Arabian Love Poems* 1992 by Bassam Frangieh and Clementina Brown.

He urged me to stay in touch and keep him posted of progress, mainly in finding a proper publisher, preferably situated in London.

After the London visit, I remained in contact with the poet – sometimes directly and sometimes through Adnan until late 1997, when he had his first heart attack. I spoke to his nurse at St. John's

Hospital in the Intensive Care Unit who told me that the poet was very ill indeed.

How does Nizar feel about poetry translation?

By the poet:

1. I don't believe in translating poetry. I don't feel enthusiastic about it. All those who have translated me murdered me, although they didn't intend to.

2. Several translations of my poetry have been issued in French, English, Spanish, Russian, Italian and Persian. I must admit to you that none of these translations resembled me, neither from a close distance, nor from afar. I wished that the translators had conveyed my flames. To my regret, they only conveyed my ashes.

3. The translators left my heart on the surgical side table, and replaced it with a heart of plastic. My beloved translators: If you love me for God's sake, keep your hands off my poems.

4. When I read my poetry in Arabic, the ballroom turns to a burning forest. When a translation is read, the ballroom turns to a freezing field and I become an Eskimo poet.

5. A year ago, I presented a reading at the Royal Opera House in Brussels. On my right there was a lady who read my poems in Flemish. On

my left, a lady who read them in French. For the first time in my life I was about to faint while sitting between Flemish Hanna and French Manna.

6. Whenever my poems are discovered by a new translator, I start reciting The Fatiha to bid farewell to my poems.

7. I wonder why some Arab poets strive to translate their poetry. As if translation will bolster their honour, fame and will book for them a place in paradise. As far as I am concerned, I don't believe in entering the English, French, Russian, Swedish and Chinese heavens. I would rather stay in the jungles of Lebanon, the topiaries of Syria, the gardens of Iraq, and the traditional neighbourhoods of Cairo. And I wonder if any Vietnamese, Kampuchean or North Korean poets would make such haste.

8. I could be capable of migrating bodily and geographically, but not linguistically.

9. My language of poetry is unexchangeable to other currencies, be it the Dollar, the Deutsche Mark or the Japanese Yen. It is also non–transferable to overseas markets. It cannot put up with expulsion and deportation. Other kinds of literature such as novels, stories, plays, memoirs and critiques could all

depart from their place of birth without losing their purity, authenticity, and national and linguistic roots. Poetry, however, wouldn't undertake this crazy adventure without losing its protective cover and base. It is unwelcome in all ports, just like a Vietnamese refugee.

10. The haste by some poets to approach Western publishers to gain the blessing of Western recognition through translation is infested with "western complex." This "complex" has been residing inside our innermost minds since colonial days.

11. All that, however, does not imply that I repudiate the West and reject extending my cultural bridges to it. Culture is a humanistic river of knowledge whose flow no one can stand against. I exclude poetry alone. Poetry is an exceptional art that cannot be deemed a commodity among those covered by the GATT treaty.

12. Poetry is a mercurial substance, highly inflammable and highly volatile. It's an explosive material that no one can control. It is always a hazardous material when it comes to packaging, processing, marketing and shipping. If it happens that it is very easy to ship preserved meat, packed food, canned fruit, the export of packaged poetry is deemed a kind of slavery.

13. I always asked myself: What would the "Wine Poems" of Abu Nawas mean to a people who have a thousand kinds of wine, like the French? What would the elegies of al-Khansa'a mean to the Brazilians who dance the Samba day and night? And what would the platonic love poems of Arab poets like Jameel of Buthaina, Kuthair of Azza and Qais bin al-Mullowah mean to peoples who resolved their sexual problems three centuries ago? Consequently, there are certain issues that we see with magnifying lenses, which the European cannot see with bare eyes.

14. My translated love poems have been fraught with *naïveté*. I write my poems to a woman from Damascus or Beirut, from Cairo or Tunis. But if I read my poems to a woman from Sweden or Denmark, no single hair would move on her body.

15. An irony of translation is that the more complicated the poem, the easier it is to translate. And the clearer it is, the more difficult it is to translate. That's why it is no wonder that modernists dance for joy when they are able now to transpose their work to languages that have neither subject and object nor syntax and not even rhyme.

16. One day I told one of my translators: I don't want you to photograph me. I want you to create me!

17. The doomed pre–Islamic poems that were translated by European Orientalists have turned to frozen corpses in the operating theatres of the academies, universities and research centres. Umrua al-Qais has become a beggar at the Sorbonne University. Al-Farazdaq looked ludicrous in his English hat. Antara bin Shaddad never tried German beer.

18. The art of rhetoric is an art exclusive to the Arabs. It cannot be exported anywhere outside the Arabian Peninsula.

19. Al-Muttanabi could appear convincing in Arabic and so could Abu Tammam, ibn al-Roomi and Tarafa bin al-abd. But if any of the above poets orated on a Sunday morning at Hyde Park, none would be applauded.

20. If the poet knows beforehand that translating his work into a second language would rank him tenth after being first in his own language, why would he then accept the demotion of his poetic rank and the reduction of his salary? Is it necessary that a poet should sweep the floors of the Kremlin in order for his work to be translated into Russian? Is it necessary that he work as a butler at the White House, so that

an American publisher would accept printing his anthology in English? Is it necessary that he work as a gardener at the Elysée Palace so that a Parisian publisher would publish his anthology in French? I personally prefer to be a good poet in my own tribe rather than a mediocre one in other tribes.

21. Perhaps introducing Arabic poetry would be important at universities and academies. But is it worthwhile that we slaughter ourselves in order to reach the table of the Western consumer? The New World Order, according to all indicators, would not care unless it benefited its economy and investments. Its strategy has no links with culture, poetry or prose, but is aimed at squeezing the last drop of our oil and blood. How ridiculous we appear when we think of exporting our poetry books to those who think only about our pockets. Let us stop cultural begging, because the International Monetary Fund (IMF) refuses to grant a ten–dollar loan to Abu al-Tayyib al-Mutanabbi!

AL–Hayat Arabic daily, Friday, 18 August 1995, Issue No. 11866, p. 20 Culture & Arts, London.

Notes to the Poems

Painting With Words:

Harun al-Rashid (c. 764–c. 809 BCE) was the fifth and most famous Abbasid caliphs. His empire included all of southwest Asia and the northern part of Africa. He was a patron of the arts, and during his reign, Baghdad was at its apogee. He figures prominently in *A Thousand and One Nights*.

Daily Love Exercises:

The **Byzantine** Empire spanned one thousand years (4th–15th century AD) and influenced the political, religious and cultural formation of near–Eastern and Western European medieval history.

The Last Declaration Of King Schariar:

The **Mythical Lover** is a name which the translator substituted for the name Qais ibn al-Mulawwah (died AD 688). Kabbani used Qais in the original poem. Qais was a "platonic" poet who was madly infatuated with Layla bint Saad. Great love stories and myths emerged about the love of the two. Qais was rejected by Layla's father. This made him lovelorn, wandering the deserts of Arabia and Syria in ghostly solitude and singing the praises of Layla until he was found dead. He was known as the *Majnun* of Layla or the mad lover of Layla (or the Crazy for Layla).

Schariar was the legendary King of Samarkand, who killed his wives in *A Thousand and One Nights*. He found that he had been deceived by his wife and as punishment had her put to death along with a succession of three thousand virgins (one each night).

You Want:

Aladdin in *A Thousand and One Nights* used to own the magical lantern or the genie lamp.

Babylon was the ancient city of Mesopotamia (now Iraq), on the Euphrates River. The brilliant colour and luxury of Babylon became legendary from the days of Nebuchadnezzar (died 562 BCE). The Hanging Gardens were one of the Seven Wonders of the world. The Persians captured the city in 538 BCE.

Cleopatra (c. 69–c. 30 BCE) was Queen of Egypt in the Pharaonic era and one of the great romantic heroines of history.

Damascene or Damascus–Syria.

Esfahan is a city in central Iran on the Zayandeh River long renowned for its fine carpets.

Khosru I (c. 531–c.579 BCE), known as Chosroes in the west, succeeded his father, Kavad, as ruler of Persia in 531. A Sassanian, he is known in eastern sources as Anushirvan (of immortal soul) because of his fame. For the Arabs, his name, rendered as Kisra, became the generic name for all the Sassanian kings. Khosru also built many palaces and castles.

Menna and Salwa are traditional Arabian delicacies.

Shehrazad was the fabled princess and wife of the Sultan Schariar in *A Thousand and One Nights*. She was a woman of exceptional intelligence, wisdom and bravery, who saved not only her life by telling a series of spellbinding tales during the dark of Arabian nights, but the lives of a dwindling supply of virgins of her country, and, by so doing, educated a King.

Sinbad was a fabled wealthy citizen of Baghdad in *A Thousand and One Nights*. He was renowned for his adventures that related his seven wonderful voyages using his magical flying mat. Also called Sind'bad.

Solomon, son of King David, was Prophet and King of Israel (c. 970–c. 928 BCE) Solomon built many palaces of gaudy splendour in the "miloh" area including one for the Pharoah's daughter. Around Solomon himself there sprang up the myth of extraordinary regal eminence and superhuman wisdom.

A Letter To An Anonymous Man:

The **Black Knight** is a term created by the translator and is used to describe the guardian and protector of a woman. In the original Arabic, Kabbani assimilated the character with that of Antara al-Absi (*see Antara al-Absi*).

Antara al-Absi (c. 525–c. AD 615) was an eminent pre–Islamic poet and warrior–knight. His mother was from Abyssinia (now Ethiopia), and gave her son his black colour. He possessed one of the seven exclusive odes *(Muallakat)* suspended around the Kaaba. He was renowned for his chivalry in the battles. Being half–caste, Antara was initially enslaved by his father until he proved to be a hero after rescuing his tribe from defeat in several battles. A number of folktales have emerged about his struggle to marry his beloved white cousin Abla.

Vessel Of Pus:

Abdul Hameed II (1842–1918) was the last sultan of the Ottoman Empire in Turkey (1876–1909). He was known as "The Great Assassin" for his part in the Armenian massacres suppressing the revolt of 1894–1896. Some books such as those of John Haslib and Georgy Zaydan portrayed him as "The Red Sultan." It presents Sultan Abdul Hameed as a man sunk into pleasures of life such as women and alcohol and a vicious merciless tyrant towards his political enemies and his people. However, some historians have regarded these books as hateful propaganda against a devout Muslim leader.

Circassian (Circassia) is the former name of the area of the North Caucasus, ceded to Russia by Turkey in 1829 and now part of the Karachai–Cherkess region of Russia.

Muttaka is Turkish–style seating with cushions.

Narghile is an Oriental tobacco pipe in which smoke is drawn through water by a long tube; hookah; hubble–bubble; Shishah; Gedu.

The Runners:

Ammoria was a Byzantine city in Asia Minor or Anatolia; the Asian part of Turkey. It was conquered by the Abbasid Muslims in 838 but now effaced.

Antakya (also known as Antioch) is located near the disputed Iskenderun Bay in the Syrian–Turkish border. The Arabs conquered it in 636 and later the Crusaders in 1098. This ancient city has an important place in Christian history since the word Christian was adopted for the first time in history in AD 40 after the followers of Nicholas of Antioch.

Notes on the other Poets:

Al-Mutanabbi (915–965), b. Iraq, is considered the greatest classical Arab poet. His early involvement with a religious cult earned him the sobriquet the would–be prophet. He was part of the brilliant court of the Hamdanid ruler Sayf al-Dawlah in Aleppo, where he wrote many of his elaborate panegyrics.

Professor Reynold A. Nicholson (1868–1945) was Sir Thomas Adams Professor of Arabic and Persian at the University of Cambridge, and a distinguished editor and translator. This artistic and scholarly translation is from his book *Translations of Eastern Poetry and Prose*, Cambridge University Press, 1987.

Octavio Paz (1914–1998) was a Mexican writer and Nobel Prize winner in literature.

References

1. Badawi, M. M., A Critical Introduction to Modern Arabic Poetry. Cambridge University Press, 1975, p. 221–222.

2. "Panoramic interview with Nizar Kabbani" *Al–Khaleej* Arabic Daily, Culture supplement, No. 6987 (July 6 1998), p.1–2.

3. "Interview with Mu'taz Kabbani", Ibid.

4. "Nizar Kabbani: Homeland around my hospital bed" *Al–Hayat*, The International Arabic Daily, Culture and Arts page, No. 12712 (December 19 1997), p. 20.

5. "Arabs bite the moon of Poetry", *Al–Hayat*, The International Arabic Daily, Culture and Arts page, No. 11866 (August, 18, 1995), p. 20.

6. *Al–A`mal Al–Shi'riyya Al–Kamila (The Complete Poetic Works),* Manshurat Nizar Kabbani, Beirut, 1970.

7. *Nizar Kabbani: Arabian Love Poems, Full Arabic and English Texts*, trans. by Bassam Frangieh and Clementina Brown. Colorado Springs, Three Continent Press, 1993.

8. Nicholson, R. A., *Translations of Eastern Poetry and Prose*, Cambridge University Press, 1987.

9. *The Huchinson Multimedia Encyclopedia, version 1.0,* Aztech New Media Corp., Ontario, 1995.

10. Fairbairn, Anne, and al-Gosaibi, Ghazi, *Feathers and the Horizon: A selection of modern poetry from across the Arab world*, The Leros Press, Duffy, 1989.

11. Jayyusi, Lena, and Elmusa, Sharif, et al, *On Entering the Sea*, Interlink Books, New York, 1996.

12. Suayah, Saadun, *Poems of Love and Exile*, Dar Sader,Beirut, 1998.

Nayef al-Kalali

Nayef al-Kalali (born 1958) is a Bahraini national and a civil engineer living and working in Manama, Bahrain. He studied for his engineering degrees in Canada and the United Kingdom. As former editor–in–chief of *Al–Mohandis*, the bilingual journal of the Bahrain Society of Engineers, Mr al-Kalali's writing background is mainly scientific. However, his passion for poetry has considerably overwhelmed his writings. He also has translated a number of unpublished works for several Arab poets in addition to his own poems.

Mr al-Kalali first met Mr Kabbani in Bahrain in December 1995, where he showed the poet the draft translation of this volume. At that encounter, Mr Kabbani initially and adamantly refused to allow his works to be translated, citing at least 21 reasons for his objection (see Mr Kabbani's article on p. 221 but he agreed to look at the draft and it was not until April 1996, while visiting London, that Mr al-Kalali was asked, through the Bahrain Embassy, to meet Mr Kabbani.

The translation was discussed further and permission granted to go ahead with the project.

Lisa Kavchak

Lisa Kavchak is a poet and novelist living in Williamsburg, Virginia, where she retired with her husband and two children after 12 years of travelling the world. Ms Kavchak and her family were resident for two years in Bahrain, where she met Mr al-Kalali and Mr Kabbani and began to work on this volume. She wishes to thank both of them for allowing her the opportunity to become immersed in Arab culture and share with them her life's love – the written word.

نــزار قبّــاني

جُمْهُـوريّة العِشْــق

مختارات شعرية مترجمة

ترجمها إلى الإنجليزية نايف عمر الكلالي

تدقيق ليزا كافشاك

كيغــان يــول إنترناشــيونال

لندن ونيويورك

For Product Safety Concerns and Information please contact our EU representative GPSR@taylorandfrancis.com
Taylor & Francis Verlag GmbH, Kaufingerstraße 24, 80331 München, Germany

www.ingramcontent.com/pod-product-compliance
Lightning Source LLC
Chambersburg PA
CBHW071523110726
47908CB00003B/928

* 9 7 8 1 1 3 8 9 8 5 1 9 3 *